Security Evaluation for Small Computer Centers

THE CHANTICO TECHNICAL MANAGEMENT SERIES

QED® Information Sciences, Inc.
Wellesley, Massachusetts

© 1985 by QED Information Sciences, Inc.
QED Plaza o P.O. Box 181
Wellesley, MA 02181

Originally published by The Chantico Publishing Company
Port Jefferson, New York

Library of Congress Number 85-60178

International Standard Book Number 0-89435-154-0

Printed in the United States of America

SECURITY EVALUATION FOR SMALL COMPUTER CENTERS

TABLE OF CONTENTS

SECURITY EVALUATION FOR SMALL COMPUTER CENTERS

TABLE OF CONTENTS (Continued)

SECURITY EVALUATION FOR SMALL COMPUTER CENTERS

TABLE OF CONTENTS (Continued)

SECURITY EVALUATION FOR SMALL COMPUTER CENTERS

TABLE OF FIGURES

SECURITY EVALUATION FOR SMALL COMPUTER CENTERS

TABLE OF FIGURES (Continued)

TABLE OF FIGURES (Continued)

SECURITY EVALUATION FOR SMALL COMPUTER CENTERS

SECTION 1

PURPOSE AND CONTENT OF THE MANUAL

SECTION OVERVIEW

This manual is concerned with the activities required to review and evaluate the security of small computer centers. It presents all the major elements to be considered in such a review.

The variety of small computer centers is discussed, and the importance of their security emphasized. The two primary objectives of an EDP security evaluation of a small computer center are:

- to assure that adequate protection is provided; and
- to make security recommendations.

The use of checklists, worksheets, and procedures provided in this manual give action-oriented direction towards the most significant problems and requirements.

The contents of the manual are briefly outlined in this section.

1

1.1   SMALL COMPUTER CENTERS

A small computer center may consist of several microcomputers, a mini-computer, a super minicomputer, or a number of different sized but relatively small computers and their related peripheral equipment, data storage facilities, documentation, and supplies. It may be in a relatively small, air conditioned room under control, or it may be a stand-alone machine without its own special room. In addition, several remote terminals, other small computers, and related equipment may be interconnected with the small computer center. Such interconnected equipment may include small business systems, scientific and engineering computers, intelligent terminals, programmable calculators, and personal computers. They will normally be located at the user site, usually for single purposes, and will operate in either detached or distributed data processing modes.

Small computer centers are essentially simply smaller and less elaborate versions of the bigger, highly-organized, and centralized computer systems operated by large organizations. Although the installation and the appearance of the small computer center does not present the overpowering effect that a large centralized computer center does, it is, nevertheless, a vital part of the operation of the organization. It is just as important to manage the security of a small computer center as it is for other, larger centers. A small computer center may handle payrolls, accounting functions, customer records, inventory, and many other items of information that are vital to the organization. As such, they should be under management control, and are subject to many of the same problems and constraints as are larger systems.

The class of computer systems in small computer centers is proliferating rapidly, because they are readily used for smaller applications, for user-controlled applications, and in the small business market. They are excellent for smaller, defined sets of programs, and as nodes in a distributed processing network. The great convenience, attractive economics, and remarkable performance of these small computer systems makes them particularly desirable to use in many applications.

The security of small computer centers should be addressed in a way similar to the security planning, implementation, management, and periodic review of the more complex centers. There are many differences, but they are more differences of complexity than of importance.

The user need not be especially knowledgeable about computers, and need not have a programming staff. The mode of operations, in many cases, is through the use of purchased programs on floppy disks. Updating of data can be accomplished manually via the CRT terminal or automatically, through the use of an interactive database system. There is strong support for high-level languages and several proven operating systems. Numerous packaged program systems are available on the market at low cost. Documentation is frequently somewhat incomplete.

1.2   SECURITY EVALUATION OF SMALL COMPUTER CENTERS

The two primary objectives of an EDP security evaluation of a small computer center are:

- **To Assure That Adequate Protection is Provided:** This consists of resources requiring protection, determining the types of potential hazards, assessing the adequacy of protective controls and devices, and continually testing the security measures. The computer system may supply and control operating data critical to the success of the rest of the organization. A review of the protection provided assures that the security measures are adequate.

- **To Make Security Recommendations:** It is impossible to foresee and prevent all potential dangers, therefore, it is necessary to periodically review the security of an operation, and to recommend control improvements. These recommendations may include methods and procedures for the operation, creation of a disaster recovery and backup plan, establishment of various physical measures, and so on.

The degree of security to be applied to a small computer center will depend upon the importance and sensitivity of the applications involved. The security aspects of a small computer system operation should be reviewed before the development and installation of the system. The primary objectives of an EDP security review is to assure that adequate protection is provided, and to make security recommendations.

Developing a good security review plan is essential to conducting an effective, efficient, and economical security review. The indentification of security risks becomes the basis of determining the adequacy of security. The risks are the requirements, so that the implemented security procedures determine how well those security requirements (i.e., security risks) have been implemented. Competent data processing systems personnel and the internal audit staff should be asked for their opinions as to what security measures to install and what policies and procedures should be followed. If the small computer system has been operating, and little thought has been given to security considerations, then a review of the operation should be conducted from the viewpoint of the adequacy of the security methods.

Extensive use is made of checklists and worksheets in this manual, as they provide a quick and reliable way to ensure that all important aspects of the review are included. They can be used for probing the critical areas associated with security planning, management, and control. They will help to determine the actual security condition rather than the perceived circumstances. These checklists and worksheets can be used either in the computer implementation planning stage or after the installed equipment has been operating. They cover the principal points of management concern relative to security. Those checklists and worksheets (or certain questions on them) that do not apply to your installation can simply be ignored, with no loss in adequate coverage.

The checklists in this manual direct the reviewer quickly to key concerns and sensitive areas. They are a good fact-gathering procedure to lead to critical areas that may have been overlooked, or which are outside the technical experience of the security officer or review team. The checklist approach minimizes the time required by the reviewers in gathering basic data, and by the personnel within the data processing organization in answering. They also provide action-oriented direction towards the most significant problems and requirements.

Through the use of the checklists, worksheets, and procedures detailed in this manual, a report can be written with the assurance that it is comprehensive in coverage. The findings from such a security evaluation of a small computer center will have come from a probe of all critical areas of management concern. Results of the evaulation will be:

a. Detailed recommendations for computer center planning or for corrective action.

b. Elimination of significant security problems.

c. A capability for continuing review of the security of distributed computer centers, stand-alone computers, and similar computerized facilities.

If the Computer Center operation is particularly sensitive, and more depth and detail is desired, it will be helpful to use the **FTP Technical Library Manual "EDP Security - Data, Facilities, Personnel, Control. "** Volume I of the manual covers Planning and Implementation, and Volume II covers Review and Testing.

1.3 CONTENTS OF THIS MANUAL

This manual on Security Evaluation for Small Computer Centers is organized as follows:

Section 2: Management Considerations - To review the planning, organizing, directing, and controlling functions of management as they are applied to the small computer center.

Section 3: Physical Security - To determine whether the computer room, the data processing area, and the surrounding building have adequate physical security measures in place, commensurate with the criticality of the systems being run there.

Section 4: Personnel Security - To assure that controls exist to minimize or avoid security breaches by both computer center and user personnel.

Section 5: Systems and Software Security - To review whether there is adequate management control in all phases of the System Development Life Cycle for both operating systems and applications software.

Section 6: Computer Operations Security Considerations - To see whether a control system is in place for all aspects of the operations, and whether adequate control points are established in sensitive areas.

Section 7: Data Communications Security - To touch on the principal technical and management concerns in the communications area.

Section 8: Control of Data Files and Vital Records To assure that the data and records that are vital to the organization and the computer system operations are adequately protected.

Section 9: User Control Responsibilities - To outline the process whereby users fulfill their responsibilities in the security of the small computer center and systems, by providing guidelines for users in establishing control objectives, and in designing, testing, and monitoring the performance of controls.

Section 10: Cost-Effectiveness of Internal Controls - To emphasize the importance of internal controls in the security protection of computer systems, and to provide a methodology for cost-effectiveness calculations.

Section 11: Analysis of Security Costs - To provide guidance for the objective analysis of the dollar costs and benefits of EDP security that are associated with the adequate control of a small computer center.

Section 12: Insurance as a Coverage - To supply worksheets and the key points in the use of insurance, in order to share risks when damage or disaster occur.

Section 13: Risk Analysis - To provide detailed checklists to aid in the assessment of probable security risks, and to help determine the adequacy of the security measures that are in place to deal with the risks involved.

Section 14: Disaster Recovery and Contingency Plans - To review the types of disasters most likely to be encountered, the variety of possible responses to disasters, the procedure for developing a sound disaster recovery plan, and the elements of disaster recovery and contingency planning procedures, in order to minimize the effects of a disaster and facilitate a rapid recovery.

SECTION 2

MANAGEMENT CONSIDERATIONS

SECTION OVERVIEW

This section provides a checklist for probing the area of the critical management problems associated with security planning, management, and control. It is concerned with the actions of all levels of management in the organization. The objective is to gain an overview of the actual security condition in the organization, rather than the perceived condition.

2.1 MANAGEMENT CONSIDERATIONS IN SECURITY EVALUATION

This section on management security considerations briefly covers the EDP management functions (planning, organizing, directing, and controlling) that provide a methodology for reviewing their effectiveness in performing those functions. If EDP management performs their functions effectively, the results of their efforts in computer security should also be performed effectively. Questions about the four functions of management could be stated as:

- Does management use planning to establish goals, objectives, and procedures for the computer operation?

- Does management direct their organization to maximize the resources available to perform the data processing function?

- Does management direct the operation in a manner that fulfills their plans?

- Does management develop and enforce the controls necessary to assure the accomplishment of the plans with a reasonable level of performance?

The checklist questions in **Figure 2-1, Management Considerations,** were developed for probing the area of the critical management problems associated with security planning, management, and control. The concern here is with the actions of all levels of management in the organization.

The objective is to gain an overview of the **actual** security condition in the organization, rather than the **perceived** condition. The responses to the checklist will be the perception of the respondents. The reviewer must compare responses from several sources, make an analysis of the actual conditions, and prepare an independent estimate of the security posture.

Figure 2-1
(Page 1)

MANAGEMENT CONSIDERATIONS

No.	Item	Responses			
		Yes	No	N/A	Comments
1.	Is user management knowledgeable about the computer system activities?				
2.	Is the organization structure clearly defined with the lines of supervision of the computer activities?				
3.	Has a central organization security administrator reviewed the security preparations for the computer operation?				
4.	Do the organization's security controls include adequate provisions for the small computer site?				
5.	Is a disaster recovery and backup operation plan included in the security plans?				
6.	Do appropriate user managers give signed approval to the security plans affecting their data processing operations?				
7.	Are all steps of hardware and software acquisition, development, and installation handled by systematic procedures with management sign-off?				
8.	Are complete and adequate Requests for Proposal prepared before any major systems acquisition?				
9.	Have the vital records of the organization been formally identified?				
10.	Have all vital records on computer media been prepared for backup and safe storage?				
11.	Are the storage locations for backup records protected from fire and adequately controlled?				
12.	Is there an adequate records retention policy which is enforced?				

Figure 2-1
(Page 2)

MANAGEMENT CONSIDERATIONS

No.	Item	Responses			
		Yes	No	N/A	Comments
13.	Are acquisition, lease, and rental contracts reviewed by legal staff?				
14.	Has the insurance coverage been assessed as to its adequacy for the computer operation?				
15.	Is proprietary and confidential software adequately protected by contracts or other legal agreements?				

SECTION 3

PHYSICAL SECURITY

SECTION OVERVIEW

A key aspect of any security review is to
determine whether the computer room and EDP
area have adequate physical security measures
in place. This section provides an outline of the
sources of information needed and a checklist
of the key physical security considerations.

3.1   <u>PHYSICAL SECURITY OF THE SMALL COMPUTER CENTER</u>

The objectives in the review of physical security include determining whether the computer room and EDP area have adequate physical security measures in place, and whether the building around it is adequately controlled and protected. Protection will include management of the inventories, access, fire protection, smoke and water protection, environmental controls, and electrical power supply. Computer equipment is subject to a number of perils which must be given consideration.

The questions in **Figure 3-1, Physical Security Considerations,** help survey the physical planning and environmental problems that affect the security planning of a data processing installation. The problems related to fire precautions will be of utmost importance to all installations. Similarly, the computer room environment is of prime importance. Reasonable precautions must be taken by prudent management in all of these areas.

●   <u>Sources of Information Needed to Review Physical Security</u>

The information required will include:

a.   Building plans, detailed in the EDP area and more general for the surrounding building and environment.

b.   Plans of utility lines, including power, telephone, water, and gas.

c.   Information about the sewer and drainage system to consider flooding possibilities.

d.   Company security procedures.

e.   Company fire manuals, including details of fire equipment, fire-fighting organization, responsibilities of individuals, actions to take when an alarm sounds, etc.

f.   Training manuals relating to security and fire control.

g.   Manufacturers' specifications and descriptions of:
   - Fire control equipment
   - Emergency alarms and lighting
   - Smoke and water detection equipment
   - Environmental controls (temperature, humidity, etc.)
   - Air conditioning systems
   - Backup power supply

If this information is gathered before a physical security review is undertaken, it can be helpful in two ways. First, it will give an indication of the overall Company security arrangements and controls in the surrounding building and environment. Data processing security procedures should always be tied into existing Company security procedures. Second, the information gathered will supply accurate answers to some of the questions on the checklist. The building and installation facts will verify and strengthen the respondents' perceptions as to the status of physical security in the area.

Figure 3-1
(Page 1)

PHYSICAL SECURITY CONSIDERATIONS

No.	Item	Responses			
		Yes	No	N/A	Comments
1.	Are there written procedures which explain the organization's security system and define the responsibilities of the personnel?				
2.	Are the entrances to the building supervised?				
3.	Are fire extinguishers provided at available locations in the areas near the computer room?				
4.	Is access to the computer room adequately controlled?				
5.	Does a solid partition surround the computer center area?				
6.	Have the employees been trained in fire-reporting and fire-fighting procedures?				
7.	Is there generally good housekeeping around the computer area?				
8.	Are there fire detection devices located in the computer area?				
9.	Is fire-fighting equipment available near the computer area?				
10.	Are appropriate fireproof safes or vaults available to store critical computer media?				
11.	Has emergency lighting been provided for the computer area that operates after the main power has been cut off?				
12.	Are there written emergency procedures that cover: a. equipment and air-conditioning power cut-off? b. requests for fire, police, and medical assistance? c. securing of data files and programs?				

Figure 3-1
(Page 2)

PHYSICAL SECURITY CONSIDERATIONS

No.	Item	Responses			
		Yes	No	N/A	Comments
13.	Are there smoke detectors in both the computer area and the computer media storage area?				
14.	Is non-combustible furniture and other equipment used around the computer area?				
15.	Is there a single-switch electrical cut-off for emergencies located separately from the computer area?				

SECTION 4

PERSONNEL SECURITY

SECTION OVERVIEW

Personnel controls are generaly administrative controls which relate to the planning and organizing functions of management. There must be procedures in place to control personnel in the area of security. This section helps to provide an indication as to the attitudes the organization has towards personnel management, training, and control.

4.1 THE CONTROL OF PERSONNEL IN THE AREA OF SECURITY

The process of determining that management's plans and directives are being followed is the process of control. Management must be assured that its desires are being met. This is as true in the handling of personnel as it is in an accounting application. Personnel controls are generally administrative controls which relate to the planning and organizing functions of management.

The control of personnel in the area of security follows the classical four steps, which are:

- Setting Standards

- Measuring Performance

- Comparing Performance against Standards

- Adjusting Standards to Reflect Changing Conditions

There must be procedures for handling these four steps in the actual practices of the organization. The objectives of the checklist questions in **Figure 4-1, Personnel Security Considerations,** are to see that these standards exist, that they are being followed, and that normal security practices are in force in dealing with the employees.

- **Sources of Information Needed to Review Personnel Security**

The information required will include:

a. Organization charts and related documents.

b. Company personnel policies, procedures, and notices relating to security. These will need to be reviewed as to their interpretation.

c. Position descriptions, particularly those relating to security management and responsibilities.

d. Employment application forms, and samples of their use, with consideration of the method and completeness of previous employer contacts and security information requests.

e. Review of the personnel records for vacation history, by employee.

f. Programs or formalized presentation of the management requirements for security, integrity, and honesty.

g. Personnel selection, testing, training methods and practice.

h. List of courses attended, and the number of days spent, by employee.

This information can be helpful in giving an indication as to the attitudes the organization has towards personnel management, training, and control. The information should supply the answers to most of the questions on the checklist, but must be verified to determine whether the written policies are actually being followed.

Figure 4-1

PERSONNEL SECURITY CONSIDERATIONS

No.	Item	Responses			
		Yes	No	N/A	Comments
1.	Do the personnel policies appear to be adequate to maintain high morale in the computer operations group?				
2.	Are personnel policies, procedures, and practices adequate to provide reliable data processing services?				
3.	Are there enforced policies requiring employees who work on financial programs to take scheduled vacations?				
4.	Are personnel in the computer area trained to cover more than one function?				
5.	Are all computer personnel familiar with their management structure and their position requirements?				
6.	Does a formal procedure exist for regular evaluation of data processing personnel performance?				
7.	Are controls established to determine that: a. programs are written according to the standards? b. systems are adequately tested prior to implementation? c. computer operations are executed according to procedures?				
8.	Are the hiring practices for computer personnel subject to the same checks and procedures required for the majority of other new employees?				
9.	If an applicant applies for hiring, is the security reliability checked with previous employers?				
10.	Is an effective EDP security training program in place and used?				

SECTION 5

SYSTEMS AND SOFTWARE SECURITY

SECTION OVERVIEW

The checklist in this section aids in the review of the adequacy of management control and security in the areas of application software, operating systems, and program changes. It is critical to examine the security control in all phases of the System Development Life Cycle. Sources of the information needed are listed.

5.1   THE REVIEW OF SYSTEMS AND SOFTWARE SECURITY

The objectives in the review of systems and software security are to determine if there is adequate management control in all phases of the System Development Life Cycle for both operating systems and applications software. Applications should be designed and developed with a formal program of management involvement and control. The form, content, completeness, and use of systems must be examined for documented control. Data management practices and controls must be adequate to maintain integrity. The checklist questions in **Figure 5-1, Systems and Software Security Considerations,** cover these concerns.

Systems and programming documentation must be protected, with controls on access to the documentation, removal and use of documentation, protection of the documentation being used, the updating of the documentation, and backup documentation procedures.

There must also be adequate standards of user interaction with all data processing activities to aid the implementation of new systems in the most straightforward manner. Only in this way will there be user satisfaction and optimum business value.

Systems and software development and use may be highly technical and most difficult to manage and control. It is critical, however, that control methods be in place and that management use them. This is particularly true in the area of the use and handling of floppy disks, which may contain all the operating and applications software, yet may be readily available to anyone in the area.

●   **Sources of Information Needed to Review Systems and Software Security**

The information required will include:

a.   Systems Development Life Cycle Standards, and an application showing its typical use

b.   Typical Functional Requirements Definition, with sufficient cost/benefit analysis to see how it is used

c.   Recent General System Design

d.   Recent Detailed System Design

e.   Programming Standards and Conventions

f.   Standards for Program Documentation, with typical program documentation

g.   Typical User Documentation and Training Documents

h.   Program Change Procedures

i.   Standards for Run Manuals, with typical Run Manual

If this information is relatively current, and if the standards and procedures are followed routinely, this information will supply the answers to the questions. It must be ascertained, however, whether the documentation represents reality.

18

Figure 5-1
(Page 1)

SYSTEMS AND SOFTWARE SECURITY CONSIDERATIONS

No.	Item	Yes	No	N/A	Comments
				Responses	
1.	Are all systems developed or acquired following a formal life cycle approach involving: a. Functional Requirements Definition? b. General System Design? c. Detailed System Design? d. Project Management and Control?				
2.	Are data security and data integrity problems considered in the designs?				
3.	Are new systems adequately tested prior to implementation?				
4.	Are procedures in effect to ensure that new application systems have the correct data structures and processing procedures?				
5.	Are all modifications and changes to programs documented and approved?				
6.	Is the programming language used specified, including constraints and special conditions?				
7.	Do on-line data entry transactions require the balancing and reconciling of input transactions and output reports by the users?				
8.	Are control functions segregated from the transaction initiation functions?				
9.	Is there adequate file control and use reporting for batch processing operations?				
10.	Are on-line systems protected from the reassignment of files by computer operators?				
11.	Is there audit trail information printed out in all financial systems?				
12.	Is a log maintained of all program versions?				
13.	Are sensitive data and programs given special protection?				

19

Figure 5-1
(Page 2)

SYSTEMS AND SOFTWARE SECURITY CONSIDERATIONS

No.	Item	Responses			
		Yes	No	N/A	Comments
14.	Are there run manuals for all operating systems containing sufficient information to: a. set-up the jobs under control? b. take action on "halt" conditions? c. verify that the output data and reports are as expected? d. review the program logic and calculations expected? e. allow correct disposition of output and files on completion of the run?				
15.	Are backup documentation files kept in safe, secure storage?				
16.	Have all files classified as critical or important been designed for reconstruction and are they backed up?				
	Operating System				
17.	Is the operating control software maintained at the most current version?				
18.	Have the control and security options and utility programs that are used been reviewed by management?				
19.	Is a disk or diskette of the operating system software stored in a secure location as backup?				
20.	Are the system utility programs used normally in application system development?				
21.	Is the program library controlled, particularly to manage personnel programs and non-standard utilities?				
22.	Are confidential or sensitive tapes copied to diskette or tape for controlled storage before they are deleted from the system?				
23.	Have the auditors assured that there are adequate controls on the operating system supplied by the vendor?				

Figure 5-1
(Page 3)

SYSTEMS AND SOFTWARE SECURITY CONSIDERATIONS

No.	Item	Responses			
		Yes	No	N/A	Comments
	Operating System (Continued)				
24.	Are the system log reports and terminal activity reports reviewed routinely to check for unauthorized use of utility programs?				
25.	Are the terminals that are not in the computer room controlled so that they can only be used to perform functions approved by management?				
26.	Is there either a manual or an automatic log kept of the system activity?				
27.	Is the operating log periodically reviewed by management?				
28.	Do procedures exist for the storage and review of the log printouts?				
29.	Do procedures exist for printing the disk history file before it overlaps itself?				
	Program Changes				
30.	Are there written procedures for authorizing, documenting, and controlling program changes?				
31.	Are the compiler and the utilities for changing source code maintained under control?				
32.	Are the source language control listings and the source language coding kept under control?				
33.	Is there a log maintained of authorized program changes?				
34.	Is there a formal procedure for making program changes, testing them, and approving them?				

SECURITY EVALUATION FOR SMALL COMPUTER CENTERS

SECTION 6

COMPUTER OPERATIONS SECURITY

SECTION OVERVIEW

A control system must be in place in all aspects
of computer operations, and control points must
be established in a variety of areas, to ensure
the security of any computer systems. This
section supplies a number of checklist questions
to cover the principal computer operations
security considerations.

6.1   SECURITY REVIEW OF COMPUTER OPERATIONS

The security review of computer operations examines the most critical area in an organization, because the computer is the funnel through which all data passes. It is in coded, or electronic, form, however, and not easily managed by supervisory personnel. The operations themselves are complex, and key points of control are handled routinely by staff actions. A control system must be in place in all aspects of the operations, and control points must be established in a variety of areas. The checklist questions in **Figure 6-1, Computer Operations Security Considerations,** deal with such controls.

a. **There must be clear computer operating instructions for all systems,** and the computer operators must be trained to follow them. The instructions must be accurate for all systems, and documented according to standards.

b. **Computer processing must be under management control** and must follow a predetermined production schedule according to standard operating methods and procedures.

c. **Adequate data controls must be in effect** through data preparation, transmission-to-data processing, key input operations, computer operations, transmission back to the user, and the handling of error conditions. The controls must be effective to prevent the loss, changing, or mishandling of data at each point of its movement through the system. All applicable methods of accounting and audit control should be considered.

d. **Adequate standards, procedures, and documentation must be prepared, in place, and observed.** The methods and procedures must ensure effective control to maintain continuous operation, to prevent processing errors, to prevent mishandling or misuse of the data, and to avoid accidental loss or destruction of data.

e. **Backup and recovery procedures must be established, documented, and controlled** to ensure that all the data is processed uniquely and correctly. All backup and recovery actions must be by predetermined procedures, which are documented, and leave a clear audit trail.

f. **Computerized data files represent the centralized collection of sensitive and critical information.** They are highly important to any organization, and they must be protected effectively. Standard handling and protection methods and procedures must be documented and followed.

23

g. Effective procedures and precautions must be managed and practiced to control and protect the personnel, equipment, software, and data in the computer facility.

h. Management must continually review the allocation and use of the data processing resources under their control. They must be concerned with capacity and cost and make rational decisions on changes. They should rely on routine job accounting and machine utilization reports that have been tested and proven.

i. The use of outside computer services should come under the same management scrutiny as the internal services. Adequate controls should be established, and trends carefully watched.

j. Operating supplies are a material part of the overall data processing costs, and they must be appropriately controlled and used. They can be critical to the overall operations, and, thus, their purchase, storage, and use should receive adequate attention.

● **Sources of Information Needed to Review Operations Security**

The sources of information needed to review operations security include:

a. **Operating Procedures**
    - Operations Standards Manual
    - Operator's Run Manuals
    - Computer Operating Procedures
    - Shift Schedules
    - Trouble Reports

b. **Control Procedures**
    - Typical Input Logs
    - Audit Reports on Controls
    - Job Accounting System Documentation
    - Utilization Reports and Trend Analysis
    - Documentation on Distribution

c. **Program Library Procedures**
    - Library or Data File Documentation and Procedures
    - List of Persons with Access to the Library or Data File

d. **Documentation**
    - Typical Application Systems Documentation
    - Typical Operating Software Systems Documentation
    - Documentation Records and Controls
    - Automated Documentation System (if any)

e. **Equipment Records**
    -   Computer Equipment Inventory List
    -   List of Hardware Features
    -   Vendor Agreements and Contracts

f. **Disaster Recovery Plans**
    -   Written Disaster Recovery or Contingency Plans
    -   Backup Site Plans
    -   Backup Agreements
    -   List of Manuals and Documentation

g. **Administration**
    -   Organization Chart
    -   Plan of Computer Room and Surrounding Areas
    -   Supplies Inventory Control System
    -   Forms Control Program

Figure 6–1
(Page 1)

COMPUTER OPERATIONS SECURITY CONSIDERATIONS

No.	Item	Yes	No	N/A	Comments
		Responses			
1.	Are the duties of the computer operator adequately separated from the data entry and control duties?				
2.	Has the computer operator been trained concerning the use and protection of confidential data?				
3.	Are there written procedures for the computer operator to follow in the event of unanticipated equipment difficulties or program running problems?				
4.	Are regular computer utilization reports routinely produced, then checked by management?				
5.	Is a job production schedule routinely prepared and followed?				
6.	Is there a regular check of the production compared to the schedule?				
7.	Is there a control procedure for the distribution of reports?				
8.	Do output reconcilement procedures provide assurance that all transactions have been computer processed?				
9.	Is the error-correction process and the re-entry of the corrected data, subject to the same control as is applied to the original data?				
10.	Is there an operations standards and procedures manual, or approved written procedures, which are adequate, up-to-date, and complete?				

Figure 6–1
(Page 2)

COMPUTER OPERATIONS SECURITY CONSIDERATIONS

No.	Item	Yes	No	N/A	Comments
11.	Do the written operating procedures include: a. operator's run manual? b. emergency actions when fire, smoke, or water alarms sound? c. handling of tapes, disks, and diskettes? d. handling problems indicated by the environmental controls? e. handling of irregular requests for work?				
12.	Are there contingency plans formalized for three levels of response to trouble: a. delay and correct situation? b. readjust schedules and possibly use some off-site equipment? c. shift to the backup computer site?				
13.	Is the working disk and diskette library kept in a locked cabinet or a separate, controlled room?				
14.	Are critical disks and diskettes identified and backed up to protect specific systems that are vital to the organization?				
15.	Have the critical jobs to be operated at the backup site, together with their datasets on disk or diskette, been identified?				
16.	Has a disaster recovery plan been developed and is each step assigned to an employee?				
17.	Have reciprocal agreements for backup of equipment been made with other organizations?				
18.	Are all files that are not scheduled for immediate use located in a separate room or in a fireproof cabinet?				
19.	Are all files prepared with both exterior and interior labels?				
20.	Is a log maintained of the use of files?				

Figure 6-1
(Page 3)

COMPUTER OPERATIONS SECURITY CONSIDERATIONS

No.	Item	Responses			
		Yes	No	N/A	Comments
21.	Are procedures adequate to control access to the computer, and to restrict it to authorized persons only?				
22.	Are operating software systems implemented only with the approval of supervisory personnel?				
23.	Are records kept of the jobs which are run on the computer?				
24.	Are the data processing supplies adequately protected and controlled?				
25.	Are the inventory control procedures for supplies adequate to assure needed inventories and to protect against unauthorized use?				

SECTION 7

DATA COMMUNICATIONS SECURITY

SECTION OVERVIEW

This section will aid in determining whether the appropriate technical analyses have been made in the area of data communications security, and whether adequate security measures are in place. A checklist is provided to aid in the coverage of the various data communications security considerations.

7.1   CONSIDERATIONS IN DATA COMMUNICATIONS SECURITY

The review suggested in this section is from the point-of-view of management control of data comunications to assure whether adequate security measures have been applied in the data communications area. There is not sufficient time in such a review to cover the details of a technical and engineering review of the data communications network and the equipment involved in it. The checklist questions in **Figure 7-1, Data Communications Security Considerations,** touch on the principal management concerns in this area.

A data communications analysis can, of course, be handled in technical detail with the appropriate tests and calculations. Management's concern, however, is to determine if such an analysis has been made by the technical personnel, and if the many factors have been considered. They must be assured that their staff is aware of the data volumes and communications costs in detail, and have considered the reasonable alternatives. The structure, size, and usage of a communications system will be critical to the degree of security control which must be imposed upon it.

Data communications is frequently the most critical area for an organization which is concerned about the possibilities of theft of assets or services, intrusion with intent to defraud, or the inflicting of disastrous damage. For this reason, the security measures to be taken should be at all levels, from locks and guards to systems and program measures.

●   **Sources of Information Needed to Review Data Communications Security**

The sources of information needed to review data communications security include:

a.   Configuration of the data communications network

b.   Communications hardware: List and details

c.   Communications software: List and details

d.   Usage of the data Communications network, such as:

- Origination and destination locations

- Frequency and times of calls

- Average and peak data rates

e.   Applications for which data communications facilities are used

f.   Public services used for communication

g.   Reports on reliability experience

h.   Security measures that have been taken

Figure 7-1

DATA COMMUNICATIONS SECURITY CONSIDERATIONS

No.	Item	Responses			
		Yes	No	N/A	Comments
1.	Is there a configuration chart showing: a. location of terminals? b. number and types of lines? c. number and types of modems? d. length of lines?				
2.	Is there a written procedure for what to do in case of problems with the: a. terminals? b. lines? c. modems?				
3.	Are specific terminals designed as "Security" terminals?				
4.	Are identification codes, passwords, or key words used, including terminal ID and operator ID?				
5.	Is sufficient audit trail material retained?				
6.	Are all junction and terminal boxes locked on the physical lines?				
7.	Are all security lines within buildings protected by conduit?				
8.	Are there written communications backup procedures?				
9.	Is there routine logging of all communicated transactions in a form that can be rapidly traced?				
10.	Is vital master information duplicated and maintained on backup files?				
11.	Are there programmed checks on the terminal operations in the applications?				
12.	Are messages checked on receipt before automatic update of master files?				

SECTION 8

CONTROL OF DATA FILES AND VITAL RECORDS

SECTION OVERVIEW

Checklist questions are given for a wide variety of considerations in the control of data files and vital records. All may not be applicable in any given situation, but all should be considered as to applicability.

8.1   DATA FILES AND VITAL RECORDS CONSIDERATIONS

The control of data and records are fundamental to computer operations but the degree of control depends on the sensitivity of the programs being run. If the programs are organizational, accounting, financial, or other control programs, the same sort of security is necessary for small computer systems as it is for larger ones.

The checklist questions in **Figure 8-1, Data Files And Vital Records Considerations,** deal with the problems of vital records.

Figure 8-1
(Page 1)

DATA FILES AND VITAL RECORDS CONSIDERATIONS

No.	Item	Responses				
		Critical	Yes	No	N/A	Comments
1.	Does each file have an internal machine-readable label with a header and a trailer record?	*				
2.	Is it possible to concurrently, but independently, update the same record in a file?					
3.	Does the system design call for: a. Frequent file dumps? b. Recording on a separate volume the altered record images?					
4.	Does the file design include the maintenance of backup data and programs?					
5.	Has protection been standardized to protect critical files against: a. Programming errors? b. Operator errors? c. System errors?					
6.	When there are many interrelated files: a. Would a transaction be processed against all files affected at one time? b. Would all transactions be batched and passed against application master files one at a time?					
7.	For files of a highly sensitive nature (especially those that are on-line), are there written rules that govern the "public and private" use of the data contained thereon?					
8.	Have files been classified as to importance, such as critical, important, useful, or nonessential?	*				

Figure 8-1
(Page 2)

DATA FILES AND VITAL RECORDS CONSIDERATIONS

No.	Item	Critical	Yes	No	N/A	Comments
		Responses				
9.	Have all files classified as critical been designed for reconstruction and backed up?	*				
10.	Are backup copies for all critical files maintained off-site:					
	a. Outside the computer center building?					
	b. Accessible with travel time of less than one hour round trip?					
	c. Served by a different munici- pal fire department unit?					
	d. Provided with assurance that only authorized personnel are allowed to enter the room where backup files are stored?					
	e. Security control entry pro- cedure rehearsed at least twice a year to assure that authorized persons, and only authorized persons, are al- lowed to enter the restricted- access room?					
11.	Are the following stored outside the computer center and systems and programming areas:	*				
	a. The three most current gener- ations of important data files?					
	b. Program library?					
	c. Operating system?					
	d. Program operating proce- dures?					
	e. Job control cards or listings?					
	f. Source decks?					
	g. Object decks?					
	h. Contingency plan?					
	i. Program documentation?					

35

Figure 8-1
(Page 3)

DATA FILES AND VITAL RECORDS CONSIDERATIONS

No.	Item	Responses				
		Critical	Yes	No	N/A	Comments
11.	Continued					
	j. For each important batch-made program of a transaction-oriented or file-updating type, a copy of the most recently executed transaction or update file, carefully and completely identified as to the exact data file and issue to which it is to be executed?	*				
12.	Is the library (i.e., the data files and program storage facilities) segregated from the remainder of the computer center in a backup or secondary storage site?					
13.	Is access to the library restricted to designated librarians?					
14.	Have operators been advised on the procedures to follow for file protection during emergencies?					
15.	Is there assurance that every disk or diskette used could be reconstructed from data in fire-resistant storage?					
16.	If magnetic files are used in open racks or shelving, is there a procedure to assure that they are duplicated in fire-resistant storage?					
17.	Are confidential documentation, files, and programs under lock-and-key protection?					
18.	Are disks, diskettes, and other data processing media, which contain confidential or restricted data, logged in and out indicating the time and person?					

Figure 8-1
(Page 4)

DATA FILES AND VITAL RECORDS CONSIDERATIONS

No.	Item	Responses				
		Critical	Yes	No	N/A	Comments
19.	Are intermediate work files (e.g., disks or diskettes used in sorts) that contain confidential data controlled to prevent improper use?					
20.	Is fire-resistant storage provided for all magnetic file media?					
21.	Does each tape file have a legible external label?					
22.	Are data files released from storage only on scheduled runs?					
23.	Is there a formal pass system in use in which no one, including computer center personnel, can remove any materials from the computer center without prior written approval of an authorized supervisor?					
24.	Have application systems been checked to see if there are files that can be merged into fewer files:					
	a. Conversely, has the application system been checked to assure that necessary redundancy between files has been provided where needed to support automated audit processes?					
	b. If a database management system is used to reduce file redundancy, has the application been checked by a qualified EDP auditor to assure that the ability to machine-generate necessary audit trails has not been inhibited by the system's file-unification processes?					

Figure 8-1
(Page 5)

DATA FILES AND VITAL RECORDS CONSIDERATIONS

No.	Item	Responses				
		Critical	Yes	No	N/A	Comments
25.	Have file retention procedures been approved by the individual charged with the responsibility for vital records maintenance?					
26.	Have these procedures been reviewed within the last year?					
27.	Is the retention cycle for the data files documented for each application?					
28.	In your opinion, is the file security adequate to handle: a. Fire emergencies? b. Theft emergencies? c. Sabotage emergencies?					

SECURITY EVALUATION FOR SMALL COMPUTER CENTERS

SECTION 9

USER CONTROL RESPONSIBILITIES

SECTION OVERVIEW

A fundamental aspect of security for small computer systems is the level of control that has been established over the development and operation of the application systems that are run on the computer.

The primary responsibility for control in an application system resides with the user. The user is responsible for the accuracy, completeness, and authorization of the data in that application system. The user must be involved in the design, implementation, maintenance and operation of application systems to fulfill this responsibility.

This section provides guidelines to senior management and users in the proper assignment and execution of user control responsibilities. The section is divided into two parts. The first part covers user responsibility during the development, implementation, and maintenance of application systems. The second part covers user responsibility during the operation of application systems.

9.1 USER CONTROL RESPONSIBILITIES DURING DEVELOPMENT

User application systems can be initiated by the user or by other parties. The user may specify the system's requirements, and develop the system utilizing internal or outside resources. The user may purchase and install a commercially developed application system to meet the specifications. The user may or may not participate in the feasibility study and development of the system.

Regardless of the initiating method, the user should be an active participant in the development, implementation, and maintenance of that system. Organization management, data processing personnel, and the user are all involved in control and preparations for security. Each has the primary responsibility for certain aspects of control. The primary and secondary responsibility for control in an application system are illustrated in **Figure 9-1, Control Responsibilities.** This figure shows whether the user, data processing, or management has the primary or secondary control responsibility for the major control tasks.

The control tasks are:

- **Approve System** - The need approval to implement or modify an application system.

- **Identify Risks** - Determine which risks pose a threat to the application system.

- **Determine Acceptable Level of Loss** - Specify the amount of loss that is acceptable for each identified risk.

- **Establish Control Objectives** - Identify the control specifications.

- **Design Controls** - Determine which controls will reduce the risk to the acceptable level of loss.

- **Implement Controls** - Implement the designed and specified controls.

- **Test Controls** - Test the implemented controls to determine that they meet specifications.

- **Monitor Controls** - Verify that the controls are functioning as specified and that control violations are properly addressed.

- **Initiate Control Changes** - Specify changes to controls wherever necessary to maintain an effective and adequate system of internal control.

The tasks and responsibilities that the user must perform in fulfilling these control responsibilities are summarized in this section specifically to aid users in the fulfillment of those responsibilities.

Figure 9-1

CONTROL RESPONSIBILITIES

CONTROL RESPONSIBILITY / CONTROL TASK	USER	DATA PROCESSING	MANAGEMENT
Identify Risks	P	S	P
Determine Acceptable Level of Loss	P		
Establish Control Objectives	P	S	
Design Controls	S	P	
Implement Controls	S	P	
Test Controls	P	S	
Monitor Controls	P	S	S
Initiate Control Changes	P	S	

P = Primary Responsibility
S = Secondary Responsibility

Approve System

Senior management has the primary responsibility to approve application systems for implementation. This responsibility may be delegated to lower levels of management, particularly the maintenance of systems.

The user has a secondary responsibility in systems approval. This responsibility is to develop specifications which are acceptable to the user, are in harmony with the plans, policies, and procedures of the organization, and are implementable at the estimated cost by data processing personnel.

Identify Risks

The user has the primary responsibility for identification of risks in their application systems. That responsibility may be at the data element level in a database environment. Data processing personnel have a secondary responsibility since certain risks are data processing-oriented risks. Risks in application of technology are a prime example.

Determine Acceptable Level of Loss

The user has primary responsibility for determining the acceptable level of loss for each risk. While the data processing department can help with risk identification, the determination of an acceptable level of loss is a sole user responsibility. Only the individual responsible for the risk can determine what level of loss is acceptable.

If the user specifies an acceptable level of loss for risks in the operation of applications, then:

- Controls can be specified to achieve those levels of loss.

- The economics of building, implementing, and monitoring controls can be determined for those acceptable levels of loss.

- The performance of the controls can be monitored to determine whether or not that acceptable level of loss is being achieved.

This manual has provided a methodology to help users determine an acceptable level of loss. This methodology is outlined in **Section 13, Risk Analysis.**

Establish Control Objectives

Once the acceptable level of loss has been established, control objectives can be specified to achieve those acceptable levels of loss. There is a close inter-relationship between establishing control objectives and determining an acceptable level of loss.

The cost of a perfectly secure system is extremely high and in most cases not achievable. Thus, the control objective of assuring that all items shipped are billed is unrealistic if it implies perfection. Users must be willing to accept less than perfection in computerized applications. If they adopt this realistic attitude, then realistic systems can be built and monitored. Users should not accept a state where the errors exceed what has been specified as "acceptable."

Design Controls

Data processing personnel have the primary responsibility for the design of controls. If the user has properly specified the control needs, this becomes a mechanical process. Problems occur when users fail to meet their specification responsibility and delegate that responsibility, usually in a de facto manner, for the data processing personnel.

Test Controls

The user has the primary responsibility to verify that the controls function according to the specifications. This does not mean that the data processing people are not actively involved in the test process. Just the opposite is true. A large segment of the time of data processing people is expended in testing computerized applications.

The user should test the system in their own operating environment. The system should run using the documentation provided by the systems development team. User personnel should attempt to operate the system, and the controls in the system, using that documentation.

The user has the responsibility to establish the control objectives, which are designed to reduce the risks to an acceptable level. The user knows best how the system should perform. For this reason, many users prepare their own acceptance test data and then test the system to determine that it meets their system specifications.

9.2   CONTROLLING OPERATIONAL SYSTEMS

The developmental phase ends when the user accepts the implemented system for operational purposes. The user has agreed that the data processing personnel have built and implemented the system they specified. The question remains as to whether it will perform in a real-world operating environment as it did in a test environment.

There are two tasks for the user to perform in monitoring application systems. These are:

● Monitor the Performance of Controls

● Initiate Control Changes Whenever Controls Fail to Achieve the Acceptable Levels of Performance

Monitor the Performance of Controls

Monitoring the performance of controls is the primary responsibility of the system user. Data processing people have a secondary responsibility in that some of the controls are data processing oriented controls. The data processing people must accept responsibility for mounting the right disk file, using the correct version of the program, and other internal data processing operating procedures.

The monitoring of controls in a computerized application involves two tasks:

- Establishing Feedback Mechanisms

- Monitoring the Information Produced by those Feedback Mechanisms

Each control should have associated with it a feedback mechanism. This feedback mechanism is a mini-report writer which provides information on the performance of the control, and about the transactions which are being controlled by it. Both are needed to effectively monitor the performance of the control.

Users should specify the methods of reporting feedback information as part of the control specifications of an application system. Users should develop the manuals and procedures needed for their personnel to incorporate this information into the monitoring process.

The following reporting and organizing alternatives are available for monitoring controls:

Feedback Reporting and Organizing Alternatives	Purpose
Listings	unstructured lists of data
Control Logs	unstructured lists of data with space to indicate action taken
Columnar Information	structured and totalled data
Trend Analysis	show changes to data
Bar Charts	compares data visually
Ratios	compares data mathematically
Comparisons/Ranking	ranks data in order of importance
Pie Charts	visually shows relationships parts and the whole
Multilevel Accumulation	shows build-up of accumulated data

Change Authorization Process

An essential element of control of the systems maintenance process is control over what changes are made. Control requires two things: first is an authorization process, and second is knowing if the process is being followed. This necessitates some type of feedback mechanism indicating what changes are, or have been made.

Normal maintenance requests occur in one of two ways. First, some type of problem occurs which requires analysis and possible correction. Second, changes occur due to changing business conditions. Both require some form of analysis and change authorization.

The user retains responsibility for the accuracy and completeness of the system and, therefore, must be the central control point. All program change requests should be approved by the user of the System. Regardless of the method by which either the problem is recognized or the change originates, the user must approve all changes.

Two forms are used by Touche Ross & Co. to record problems and request changes. These copyrighted forms are reproduced in the manual by permission of Touche Ross & Co. Examination of these forms, and the procedures for completing them, will provide an understanding of the type of information needed.

Problem/Request Control Form

The Problem/Request Control Form enables individuals to document problems that they perceive in a computerized application. The problem is normally sent to the data processing personnel, who determine the reason for the problem. The data processing personnel, in conjunction with the user, will normally develop a solution or determine an acceptable disposition to the problem. If the solution requires a change to the computerized application, then the Change Request Form is completed.

The following is the purpose and procedures explanation relating to the **Problem/Request Control Form** (Form No. 33), which is illustrated in **Figure 9-2.**

| Purpose: | To record problems and changes to a system once it is past system testing. |

Procedure for Completing:

Information	Action
1. Heading	Complete and check appropriate boxes.
2. Symptom/Request	Indicate the description of the symptom on change request. Sign and date.
3. Problem/Reason	Indicate the description of the problem on change modification. Sign and date.
4. Solution/Disposition	Indicate the description of the solution or disposition. Sign and date.

45

Figure 9-2

PROBLEM/REQUEST CONTROL FORM

PAGE _____ OF _____

PROJECT NO. _____

Touche Ross
Organization _____   Priority _____   Prepared By _____
                            Number _____   Reviewed By _____
System _____   Commitment Date _____   Date   _____
User Rep. _____   Complete? ___ Date _____   Phase   _____

System/Request
Submitted By   Date

Problem/Reason
Diagnosed By   Date

Solution/Disposition
Solved By   Date

CHANGE REQUEST(S) ISSUED

No.	Item To Be Changed	Assigned To	Date Required	Date Of Actual Completion

Approved By   Date

5.	Change Request(s) Issued	Indicate the number, item to be changed, assigned to, date required. Also fill in a Change Request Form (Form No. 34). Sign and date.
6.	Date of Completion.	Indicate the date this item was completed.

Change Request Form

Either a problem uncovered, or a change in business procedures, can necessitate a change to a computerized application. The needed change should be documented on a Change Request Form (Form No. 34). This form is normally prepared by the data processing personnel in conjunction with the user department. In some organizations, the user department prepares the form. In all cases, the user should approve the change.

A review of the form and the procedures will provide an understanding of the type of information and action taken on a Program Change Request. The form is illustrated in Figure 9-3. The following information explains the purpose of the Change Request Form, together with the procedures for completing the form.

<u>Purpose:</u>	To communicate to various responsible parties a change that must be made to a system that is past system test.

Procedure For Completing:

	Information	Action
1.	Heading	Complete and check appropriate boxes.
2.	Reason for Change	Indicate a description for the <u>reason</u> for the change.
3.	Description of Change	Indicate a description of the change.
4.	Documentation Attached	Indicate the documentation which is attached.
5.	Changes Required	Complete the appropriate items.
6.	Comments	Indicate comments as appropriate.
7.	Signature and Date	Sign and date.

Figure 9-3

CHANGE REQUEST FORM

PAGE _____ OF _____

PROJECT NO. _____

Touche Ross   No. _____

Organization _____   Problem/Request No. _____   Prepared By _____

                    Assigned To _____   Reviewed By _____

System _____   Date Required _____   Date

User Rep. _____   Complete? ____ Date _____   Phase   _____

Reason For Change

Description Of Change

Documentation Attached

Changes Required

Item	Performed By	Date Completed		Item	Performed By	Date Completed
Program			__	Run Instructions	_____	_____
Program Documentation	_____	_____	__	User Procedures	_____	_____
File	_____	_____	__	_____	_____	_____
File Documentation	_____	_____	__	_____	_____	_____
Printer Layout	_____	_____	__	_____	_____	_____
Data Element Dictionary	_____	_____	__	_____	_____	_____
Test Data & Run	_____	_____	__	_____	_____	_____

Comments

Requested By	Date	Changed By	Date	Approved By	Date
_____	_____	_____	_____	_____	_____

SECTION 10

COST-EFFECTIVENESS OF INTERNAL CONTROLS

SECTION OVERVIEW

Internal controls are one of the strongest measures that can be taken in the security protection of computer systems. It is mandatory to establish sufficient controls on a cost-effective basis to protect the assets represented in data processing systems. Based on articles in the press, however, it appears that there are clearly insufficient controls placed on the operation of small computer systems.

This section addresses an approach to the identification of controls and the estimation of their costs and benefits. It suggests that controls be identified that achieve a specific control objective for the cost-effectiveness calculations. Useful forms are provided for these cost-effectiveness calculations, and a number of tables are included that suggest possible costs and benefits that may be considered in the analysis.

10.1 COST-EFFECTIVENESS OF CONTROLS ON SYSTEMS

Internal accounting controls are one of the strongest measures that can be taken in the security protection of computer systems. While physical security and the control of personnel are of utmost importance in maintaining a secure operation, the fundamental assurance of the security of the assets represented in the application programs lies in the internal systems controls that are established in the systems design and programming. All of the types of security controls mentioned in this manual are desirable, and some are necessary. Internal accounting controls, however, should be mandatory.

The Foreign Corrupt Practices Act of 1977 requires organizations to establish internal accounting controls on a cost-effective basis. While traditionally controls have been established for material, it is now generally accepted that controls must be equally established for all assets represented in data processing systems. It is apparent from articles in the press in recent years that there are insufficient controls on most small computer systems and communications networks. There has been wide publicity about program "piracy", and about groups of computer users and "hackers" breaking into and altering systems, and of outright theft. Only the tip of the iceberg of loss of assets to organizations has been exposed.

Internal accounting controls are necessary. Establishing their cost-effectiveness may be quite difficult, however, as in large systems there may be literally thousands of controls that perform in concert. How many are truly required? Despite the problems of addressing this issue, an attempt should be made to do so systematically. All that is known about the costs and benefits of single controls or groups of controls should be stated as objectively as possible for management consideration. This section addresses an approach to such identification and estimation that can be used to describe both overall values and specific values of controls.

The prerequisite to calculating the cost-effectiveness of controls is to identify the controls to be considered. It is easy to identify the controls, but it is difficult to identify those controls that are significant for making a meaningful cost-effectiveness analysis.

Four approaches that can be used for identifying controls are:

- **Identify Individual Controls** - Each individual control is identified as a control. For example, individual controls would be the pre-printed number on a check, the supervisor's signature on a timecard, the programmed edit that verifies an employee number is acceptable.

- **Identify Key Controls** - These are those controls identified as the more important controls in an application system.

- **Identify Cluster of Controls** - These are all of the controls performed by a single individual, located within a single function, physical location, or segment of a computerized application.

- **Identify Controls That Achieve A Control Objective** - The group of controls designed to achieve stated control objectives. For example, if the control objective is to ensure that all shipments are billed, then all of the controls necessary to achieve this objective are considered a single subsystem or family of controls.

Any or all of these definitions of control can form the basis of a cost-effectiveness analysis. Of the four, identifying individual controls is the least effective, because there are large amounts of individual controls. The key control identification appears to be a good method, but fails to take into account compensating or secondary controls that help achieve control. The cluster of control method of identification is most valuable in estimating the cost of a large number of closely related controls.

The recommended method for identifying controls is to group together for analysis purposes **all of those controls related to a single control objective.** Thus, the control objective becomes the focal point for the cost-effectiveness calculation. In estimating the costs associated with the control objective, grouping controls into one or more clusters may make cost estimation much easier and more economical. When objectives are used, benefits calculations become much easier to quantify and explain.

This material is extracted from the FTP Technical Library manual, Internal Controls. It is more fully described in that manual.

10.2   COST-EFFECTIVENESS CALCULATION FORMS

The methodology for determining the cost-effectiveness of a control objective is summarized into three worksheets. The first is a summary worksheet identifying the control objectives with the related information necessary to develop a decision regarding the implementation or non-implementation of controls **Figure 10-1, Cost-Effectiveness Calculation Worksheet.** The decision process uses cost and benefit information, but still requires human judgment.

The second worksheet is used to develop the costs associated with implementing a control **Figure 10-2, Control Cost Worksheet.** The third worksheet is used in developing the benefits associated with the implementation of controls **(Figure 10-3, Benefits Worksheet.** These worksheets provide the cost and benefit information which is then transcribed to the summary form.

Cost-Effectiveness Calculation Worksheet

The Cost-Effectiveness Calculation Worksheet (Figure 10-1) summarizes the cost-effectiveness calculation. The worksheet provides the necessary documentation to support the control implementation decision.

The information to be included on the form is:

- **Identification Number** - A unique number tying together the three cost-effectiveness calculation worksheets.

- **Control Objective** - The control objective on which the cost-effectiveness is being performed.

Figure 10-1

COST-EFFECTIVENESS CALCULATION WORKSHEET

	IDENTIFICATION NUMBER:
CONTROL OBJECTIVE	
KEY FIELDS CONTROLLED	
IDENTIFIED RISKS	
ACCEPTABLE LEVEL OF LOSS	
COSTS	
BENEFITS	
CONTROL IMPLEMENTATION DECISION	

PREPARED BY:	DATE:	APPROVED BY:

Figure 10-2

CONTROL COST WORKSHEET

	IDENTIFICATION NUMBER:
GENERIC CONTROLS	
DESCRIPTION OF CONTROLS	
COSTS	
Origination Costs	
Input Costs	
Process Costs	
Storage Costs	
Output Costs	
Use Costs	
PREPARED BY:	**DATE:**	**APPROVED BY:**

Figure 10-3

BENEFITS WORKSHEET

	IDENTIFICATION NUMBER:	
CONTROL OBJECTIVE		
INCOME		
COST REDUCTIONS - TANGIBLE		
People Costs		
Other Costs		
COST REDUCTIONS - INTANGIBLE		
People Costs		
Other Costs		
COST AVOIDANCE - INTANGIBLE		
People Costs		
Other Costs		
COST AVOIDANCE - INTANGIBLE		
People Costs		
Other Costs		
PREPARED BY:	DATE:	APPROVED BY:

- **Key Fields Controlled** - The actual implementation of the control will occur on key fields. The individual designing the controls builds controls around these key fields.

- **Identified Risks** - Risks are the opposite of control objectives. The purpose of identifying the risks is to be assured that the controls will, in fact, prevent the risk from occurring, and thus assure that the control objective will be achieved. Developing a detailed list of risks will help in the control of the design process.

- **Acceptable Level of Loss** - Controls cannot be designed until an acceptable level of loss is determined. The individual responsible must state what level of loss is acceptable, so that a realistic system of controls can be developed.

- **Costs** - These costs come from Figure 10-2 - Control Cost Worksheet.

- **Benefits** - The benefits come from Figure 10-3 - Benefits Worksheet.

- **Control Implementation Decision** - This contains a brief synopsis of the decision process, the decision made, and why that decision was made. This is extremely important should the decision be made not to implement controls over this control objective or sub-objective.

- **Prepared by** - The name of the individual responsible for completing the worksheet.

- **Date** - The control implementation decision date.

- **Approval** - The individual accountable for achieving the stated control objective should concur with the control implementation decision.

Control Cost Worksheet

The **Control Cost Worksheet** (**Figure 10-2**) can be used as an aid in calculating the cost of controls. The objective of the worksheet is to help organize the collection and presentation of costs associated with achieving a control objective. Prior to completing this worksheet, the controls that are proposed for implementation to achieve the control objective, must be determined.

The information to be included on the form is:

- **Identification Number** - A unique number tying together the three cost-effectiveness calculation worksheets.

- **Generic Controls** - The specific control solution recommended to achieve the stated control objectives. It is recommended that generic controls be used so that there is a consistency and readability among the various forms.

- **Description of Controls** - This section of the worksheet provides space to describe the actual implementation of the generic control.

- **Costs** - Six categories of cost are recommended, which coincide with the flow of key fields through application systems. The six cost categories are:

  - Origination costs
  - Input costs
  - Process costs
  - Storage costs
  - Output costs
  - Use costs

- **Prepared by** - The name of the individual who completed the form.

- **Date** - The date the form was completed.

- **Total cost** - The sum of all the costs listed in the cost section of this worksheet.

Benefits Worksheet

The **Benefits Worksheet** (Figure 10-3) is designed to quantify the benefits associated with implementing a control objective. The worksheet is oriented to lead the individual doing the cost-effectivenss calculation through the benefit side of the analysis.

The benefits received should be obtained through the implementation of the control objective. Therefore, the control objective becomes the center of the benefit analysis process. Normally the individual working with the form would interview or work with people knowledgeable in the application.

The information to be included on the form is:

- **Identification Number** - A unique number tying together the three cost-effectiveness calculation worksheets.

- **Control Objective** - The control objective for which the cost-effectiveness calculation is being performed.

- **Income** - The amount of revenue possibly generated as a result of implementing this control objective.

- **Cost Reductions (tangible)** - The reduction in cost that can be directly tied to achieving this control objective, such as reduction in people time.

- **Cost Reductions (intangible)** - Costs that are related to the implementation of the control objective, but cannot be directly tied to the control objective.

- **Cost Avoidance (tangible)** - Actual costs that will not be expended because a control is implemented.

- **Cost Avoidance (intangible)** - These are costs avoided which are not directly related to the implementation of a control objective but need to be considered.

- **Prepared by** - The name of the individual who completed the Benefits Worksheet.

- **Date** - The date the Benefits Worksheet was completed.

- **Total Benefits** - The total dollar amount associated with all the categories of benefits.

Many of the intangible costs can be calculated using the risk analysis concepts presented in Section 13.

10.3   DETERMINING COSTS

This section includes six tables (Figures 10-4 through 10-9), one for each of the categories of cost. Each of these tables lists possible costs associated with that category. In addition to the description of the cost is a suggested method of measuring the cost. If personnel time is the cost to be considered, then the measurement might be the dollar cost of salary plus benefits. The items included in each of the tables are meant as guides for consideration, and not costs that must be included in each control calculation.

Each control situation will be unique. It must be evaluated independently. In these evaluations, certain costs will be associated with achieving one control objective, but not with another control objective. The cost factors included in the following tables are not intended to be all-inclusive, but, rather, representative of the more typical costs to be considered in a cost calculation.

10.4   ESTIMATING BENEFITS

Organizations normally have more difficulty in estimating benefits than in calculating costs. There is often a higher degree of precision used in cost estimation than in benefit estimation. Performing the cost-effectiveness calculation in this manner leads to reliance on costs, but disbelief on benefits. For example, if costs are estimated to be $12,318, and benefits an even $25,000, a person looking at those figures would assume a lot of effort has been put into costs, but little into benefit. It is necessary to estimate costs and benefits with the same precision. If benefits cannot be estimated, then it is not worth the effort to attempt to quantify costs.

Figure 10-4

ORIGINATION COSTS

Cost Factor	Measurement for Pricing the Cost Factor
Forms	Reproduction Cost
Telephone	Telephone Company Charges
Postage	Postage Charges
Personnel	Wages Plus Benefits
Manuals	Cost to Print and Disseminate
Education/Training	Cost of Education
Hardware	Rentals or Purchase Charges
Space	Rental Cost or Equivalent
Vendor Maintenance Support	Actual Charges

Figure 10-5

INPUT COSTS

Cost Factor	Measurement for Pricing the Cost Factor
Input Device	Rental or Purchase Costs
Input Media	Purchase Cost or Depreciation
Personnel	Wages Plus Benefits
Communications	Communication Charges
Space	Rental Cost or Equivalent
Education/Training	Cost of Education
Hardware	Rentals or Purchase Charges
Vendor Maintenance Support	Actual Charges

Figure 10-6

PROCESS COSTS

Cost Factor	Measurement for Pricing the Cost Factor
Hardware	Rental or Purchase Costs
Software	Rental or Purchase Costs
Unused Capacity	Percent of Total Capacity
Education/Training	Cost of Education
Space	Rental Cost or Equivalent
Vendor Maintenance Support	Actual Charges
Personnel	Wages Plus Benefits

Figure 10-7

STORAGE COSTS

Cost Factor	Measurement for Pricing the Cost Factor
Storage Devices	Rental or Purchase Cost
Storage Library	Rental or Equivalent Cost
Backup Storage Facilities	Rental or Equivalent Cost
Messenger Service To Backup Facilities	Actual Charges
Education/Training	Cost of Education
Hardware	Rental or Purchase Charges
Destruction of Stored Media	Actual Charges
Space	Rental Cost or Equivalent
Vendor Maintenance Support	Actual Charges
Personnel	Wages Plus Benefits

Figure 10-8

OUTPUT COSTS

Cost Factor	Measurement for Pricing the Cost Factor
Hardware	Purchase or Rental Costs
Output Paper and Forms	Actual Cost
Output Software	Purchase or Rental Costs
Space	Rental or Equivalent
Personnel	Wages Plus Benefits
Education/Training	Cost of Education
Vendor Maintenance Support	Actual Charges

Figure 10-9

USE COSTS

Cost Factor	Measurement for Pricing the Cost Factor
Forms	Reproduction Cost
Communication	Actual Communications Charges
Postage	Postage Charges
Personnel	Wages Plus Benefits
Manuals	Cost to Print and Disseminate
Education/Training	Cost of Education
Hardware	Rental or Purchase Charges
Space	Rental Cost or Equivalent
Vendor Maintenance Support	Actual Charges

A common method for measuring intangible costs is risk analysis. The procedures outlined in Section 13 should prove helpful in quantifying some of the difficult to quantify benefits, such as increased customer service, more reliance on reports, increased confidence of management, etc. These are worth something, but are hard to quantify without a tool like risk analysis.

This section includes five tables (**Figures 10-10 through 10-14**) outlining the benefit factors for each of the five categories of benefits. The benefit factors are not meant to be exhaustive, nor will all of them be used in every benefit calculation. They are provided as a representative sample of the types of benefits that should be considered in each category. Associated with the benefits is a suggested method of measuring the dollar amount of benefits.

Figure 10-10

INCOME BENEFITS

Benefit Factors	Measurement for Pricing the Benefit Factor
Additional Sales of Products	Actual Profit from Sales
Rental of Unused Capacity	Actual Rental
Sale of Scrap	Actual Sales Receipts
Resale of Developed Software	Actual Receipts (assumes the organization is not in the business of selling software)
Competitive Advantage	Value of Increased Business
Increased Customer Service	Value of Increased Business
Effectiveness/Efficiency	Increased Production Value

Figure 10-11

COST REDUCTION – TANGIBLE BENEFITS

Benefit Factors	Measurement for Pricing the Benefit Factor
Personnel Reduction	Wages Plus Benefits
Space	Rental or Equivalent Reduction
Material and Equipment Reduced or Eliminated	Actual Savings
Inventory Reduction	Actual Amount of Reduction
Financial Savings	The Cost of Borrowing the Equivalent Amount of Money
Software	Rental or Purchase Price of Software Reduced or Eliminated
Hardware	Rental or Purchase Price of Hardware Reduced or Eliminated

Figure 10-12

COST REDUCTION - INTANGIBLE BENEFITS

Benefit Factors	Measurement for Pricing the Benefit Factor
Security/Privacy	Value of Material Not Lost Due to Increased Controls and/or Protection
Overhead	Cost Reduction Amounts (usually a percent of tangible reductions)
Timeliness	Cost Saved Due to More Timely Information
New Information	Cost Saved Due to Getting Better Information

Figure 10-13

COST AVOIDANCE - TANGIBLE BENEFITS

Benefit Factors	Measurement for Pricing the Benefit Factor
Personnel	Wage Plus Benefit of People Not Hired
Space	Rental or Equivalent Cost of Space Not Needed
Material/Machines	Value of Material/Machines Not Needed
Supplies	Value of Supplies Not Needed
Hardware	Rental or Purchase Price of Hardware Not Needed
Software	Rental or Purchase Price of Software Not Needed

Figure 10-14

COST AVOIDANCE - INTANGIBLE BENEFITS

Benefit Factors	Measurement for Pricing the Benefit Factor
Overhead	Cost Reducation Amounts (usually a percentage of tangible cost avoidance amount)

10.5   COST/BENEFIT DECISION PROCESS

When the cost and benefits have been determined, the necessary facts are available to make the decision. The final decision may be very obvious. If the costs significantly exceed the benefits, the control probably should not be implemented. When the benefits significantly exceed the costs, the controls probably should be implemented. It is in those cases where cost and benefits are almost equal that the difficult decisions have to be made.

Due to the normal imprecision of estimating, the dollar amount estimated should probably be assumed to be a range. A reasonable range would be plus or minus 10%. For example, if an estimated cost or benefit was caluculated to be $10,000, then for decision-making purposes it should be considered in the range of $9,000-$11,000 (i.e., plus or minus 10%).

Many factors are involved in the decision process. Cost/benefit is only one of those factors, but should be a significant factor.

SECTION 11

ANALYSIS OF SECURITY COSTS

SECTION OVERVIEW

Some security measures are mandatory as they are required by law or are needed to protect the life and well-being of the personnel. Other security measures are absolutely necessary to protect the viability of the organization. Other security measures are highly desirable for the profitable operation of the organization and the prevention of disruption. In all these cases, security should be cost-effective. When the cost of security exceeds the perceived benefits to be received, new methods of handling security should be explored. Unfortunately, many organizations are unaware of either the dollar cost of security or of the dollar value of security benefits. Without this information, intelligent decisions about security cannot be made.

This section provides guidance for the objective analysis of the dollar cost and benefits of EDP security. The criteria for costs and benefits are discussed. Worksheets are provided to perform the calculations. They may be readily adapted to particular situations.

If a more analytical approach is desired with more careful attention paid to the analysis of the organization's exposure, the probability of occurrence of events, and the dollar estimation of the risks involved, the Risk Identification and Analysis procedures should be followed as described in **FTP's manual, "EDP Security: Volume I".**

11.1   ANALYSIS OF SECURITY COSTS

In a study of security, a number of good plans and desirable measures will likely be proposed. An analysis should be made to compare the costs of these measures with the probable costs of disruption to the organization.

First, the possible disruptions must be considered and analyzed as to their probability of occurrence. Second, each specific security measure designed to forestall these disruption costs and their security alternatives may be presented for comparison in either tabular form or by Discounted Cash Flow calculations. All assumptions of probability of occurrence should be stated. Finally, and most importantly, the data processing manager must decide his preferences and order of priorities, then present his conclusions as a recommendation. Forms are provided to aid in performing this series of study steps.

The possible disruptions within the data processing area, their probability of occurrence, and their probable costs can be estimated with some degree of consistency by the data processing manager. Opinions from all management within the Information Organization should be requested and considered.

In discussing the probability of disruptions and the probable costs with user management, a serious problem will normally arise. The probable costs given by different users will not be directly comparable since they will be based on different assumptions. Some users will plead importance but will have no wish to pay for security. Other users will underestimate the catastrophe to their operations in the event of a major data processing breakdown. Still other users will ask for high reliability and will back up their requests with sufficient available funds.

The data processing manager must, therefore, resort to an analytical state-ment of the problem. He should list the probability of occurrence of disruption as it is given, the probable costs, and the costs of security solutions as he sees them. To help prepare this analysis systematically and to aid in visualizing the problem, three worksheets are included.

11.2   PROBABILITY OF OCCURRENCE

The **Probability of Occurrence Worksheet (Figure 11-1)** is intended to rate and compare, by type of asset, the probability of occurrence of security violations for each of several threats. Determination of the potential cost of security violations for each of the categories of assets is then the objective of the Probable Economic Loss Worksheet.

The objective of these two worksheets is to facilitate determination of the areas of greatest exposure. In areas where probability of occurrence and economic loss combine to produce great potential business exposure, prime consideration must be given.

Figure 11-1

PROBABILITY OF OCCURRENCE WORKSHEET

Asset	Destruction	Fraud, Theft, Embezzlement	Error	Disclosure
EDP Equipment				
Installation Facility				
Data				
Programs and System Operating				
Documentation				

Probability of Occurrence Codes: (Enter in Boxes)

1. High Probability

2. Medium Probability

3. Low Probability

Assumptions Made of Probability of Occurrence:

Definition of Terms

- **Destruction:** Refers to loss from employee accidents, natural causes (e.g., flood, fire, earthquake), malicious mischief, and sabotage.

- **Fraud, Theft, and Embezzlement:** Covers the deliberate alteration of data and programs (e.g., modification of tapes, disk packs, card files, etc.) plus the removal of physical objects (e.g., tape reels, check forms, printouts, etc.).

- **Error:** Includes losses resulting from inadequate procedures or systems design, as well as carelessness or indifference by employees. The items particularly susceptible to this problem are data and programs.

- **Disclosure:** Occurs when data or programs become available to persons lacking authorization to access the information. Unauthorized access to data or programs can either be accidental or intentional.

- **EDP Equipment:** This term includes computer mainframes, peripherals, communications, EAM, data entry, and related equipment.

- **Installation Facility:** This is defined as the total computer center other than the EDP equipment. It includes the computer and key entry room and library, lighting, air conditioning, wiring, furniture, fixtures, bursters, related ancillary equipment, supplies, forms, tapes, disk packs, punched cards (but not the replacement cost of the data or programs contained in these media) and related support facilities.

Definition of other assets is considered to be unnecessary as the terms are self-explanatory.

Instructions for Completion of Worksheet

For the Destruction, Fraud/Theft/Embezzlement, Error, and Disclosure columns, indentify the probability of occurrence by selecting the appropriate code from the following table. For example, if a high probability for destruction exists for data, enter a "1" in the appropriate box.

Probability of Occurrence Codes:

High Probability   (1)

Medium Probability   (2)

Low Probability   (3)

The form has space for stating the assumptions made in determining the probability of occurrence. This will point up the critical problems for the study group.

In one sense, filling out this form is an exercise to crystalize the thinking of the study group and to get them concerned with the more probable problems. It is also used to get a consistent set of multiplying factors in determining the areas of greatest exposure.

11.3   PROBABLE ECONOMIC LOSS

The **Probable Economic Loss Worksheet** (**Figure 11-2)** is used to determine the potential cost of security breaches for each of the categories of assets.

The financial loss of EDP Equipment, Installation Facility, Data, Programs and Operating Systems, and Documentation is to be determined both for Replacement/Reconstruction and for Performance Failure Loss. Admittedly, the definition of dollar losses from control violations is difficult. It is possible to estimate the order of magnitude of the financial penalty, however. It is not necessary to develop a finite calculation when a reasonable estimate can be made. The main purpose is to emphasize the areas of concern and to put the problems in a financial perspective.

General

All figures are to be reported in thousands of dollars and are to be determined without consideration of potential insurance recovery.

If the Replacement/Reconstruction Cost, Extra Expense, or the Business Interruption Loss is very difficult to calculate, but the sum clearly is of major proportions, the term "catastrophic" may be substituted for a specific amount. The option to use this term should be exercised sparingly.

The intent of the Replacement/Reconstruction Cost portion of the form is to state the costs required to replace or restore the destroyed asset. The cost to regain full operational status when recovery is facilitated by backup resources may be different from the cost to replace or restore the asset without the protection provided by a backup facility.

The intent of the Performance Failure Loss portion of the form is to obtain information concerning the consequences of destruction or loss of all or part of the data processing function including:

- Information on the length of time it will take to regain full operational status for the data processing function or estimated time to recover (ETR).

- The extra expense that would be incurred in the event of destruction (EE).

- The financial loss that would result from the inability to conduct the company's normal business operations or business interruption loss (BIL).

Figure 11-2

PROBABLE ECONOMIC LOSS WORKSHEET
(Dollars in Thousands)

	Replacement or Reconstruction Cost		Performance Failure Loss											
	Without Backup	With Backup	Without Backup			Current Backup			Desired Backup		
			ETR	EE	BIL	ETR	EE	BIL	ETR	EE	BIL
EDP Equipment											
Installation Facility											
Data											
Programs & Operating System											
Documentation											
Total											

Note: ETR: Estimated Time to Recover (Days)   EE: Extra Expense($000)   BIL: Business Interruption Loss ($000)

Desired Backup: (In this space identify the Desired Backup capability with one-time cost plus annual continuing cost).

75

The cost of replacing or reconstructing the several categories of assets (e.g., EDP equipment) should not be included in the Performance or Failure Loss section of the form. These calculations have been determined in the preceding two columns, Figure 11-2, Replacement or Reconstruction Cost. This section attempts to determine only the effect of destruction on the ongoing performance of the business. Calculation of Performance or Failure Loss is to be made under three different assumptions: without backup, current backup, and desired backup.

Definition of Terms

- **Without Backup:** The backup facility for each of the categories of assets (e.g., EDP Equipment) either does not exist, does not function, or, for any reason, fails to provide the recovery capability that it was intended to furnish. For example, assume that the data in the secondary storage facility was totally destroyed along with the data in the regular library. The data must then be reconstructed from source documents as there is no backup file.

- **Current Backup:** The current backup facility provides only the recovery capability that it was designed to furnish. For example, if an agreement with another installation had been made to provide computer time equivalent to 50% of your current work load, assume that the agreement will be honored.

- **Desired Backup:** This assumption represents the reasonable, cost-effective level of recovery capability you would like to achieve. For example, if you currently do not have a secondary storage facility for Data, Programs and Operating System, and Documentation, assume this facility has been created and that the aforementioned materials are fully protected in this storage facility for backup purposes.

Each of the three levels of backup has three sub-columns:

- **ETR (Estimated Time to Recover):** The lapsed time (in days) that it is estimated it will take to fully replace the asset (e.g., data) with the given level of backup.

- **EE (Extra Expense):** The necessary additional cost (expressed in thousands of dollars) required to continue the operations of the business immediately following the destruction of an asset.

- **BIL (Business Interruption Loss):** The financial loss (expressed in thousands of dollars) resulting from the inability to conduct the company's normal business operations as the result of the destruction of an asset. For example, if a customer order processing system is inoperative because of loss of the programs, this event would have an impact on the profitability of the company.

Instructions for Completion of Worksheet

a. ### Replacement or Reconstruction Cost Without Backup

Identify the costs, expressed in thousands of dollars, for:

- **EDP Equipment:** To replace all existing hardware.

- **Installation Facility:** To completely rebuild or relocate the installation.

- **Data:** To reconstruct all data files from source documents.

- **Programs and Operating System:** To write, compile, and test all programs from scratch.

- **Documentation:** To create anew all flow charts, record layouts, etc.

b. ### Replacement or Reconstruction Cost With Backup

Identify the costs, expressed in thousands of dollars, for:

- **EDP Equipment and Installation Facility:** To replace all existing hardware or rebuild the installation with no particular time pressure, and with the capability operating continuously.

- **Data, Programs, Operating System, and Documentation:** To become fully operational in each category if a satisfactory secondary (backup) storage site has been established to house copies of the data, programs, operating system, and documentation.

If there are no clear differences, the figures in the "Without Backup" column can be repeated in the "With Backup" column.

c. ### Performance Failure Loss Without Backup

For these columns, assume that each of the assets has been destroyed, is not available, or does not function because provisions for backup were not made or failed to provide any recovery capabilities.

- **ETR (Estimated Time to Recover)**

  Identify the number of days it would take:

  - **EDP Equipment:** For the vendor to replace all EDP equipment.

  - **Installation Facility:** To rebuild or relocate the installation at a new site.

77

- **Data:** To reconstruct all data files from source documents.

- **Programs:** To write, compile, and test all programs, starting from the point records are not backed up.

- **EE (Extra Expense)**

  - **EDP Equipment:** The overtime costs of clerical personnel, hiring of temporary workers, etc., to perform the entire computer's work load or that portion that could be feasibly accomplished for the time period required to replace the equipment.

  - **Installation Facility:** The costs of temporary facilities until such time when the original installation facility is restored. Also, the costs of transportation, meals, housing, security, etc.

  - **Data:** The overtime costs of clerical personnel, hiring temporary workers, etc., to overcome the problems resulting from the lack of machine-readable data until at least half of the data files can be reconstructed from source documents. Note that the EDP equipment is functioning during this time period so the cost of "duplicating" the computer work does not have to be included.

  - **Programs and Operating System:** The same type of costs as incurred for EDP Equipment destruction for half the period required to complete all programs, plus the costs resulting from having clerical personnel working with simple listings of data files until half of the programs have been completed.

  - **Documentation:** The additional costs of systems analysis and programming in changing systems and programs as the result of the lack of documentation for half the time period required to complete the recreation of the documentation.

- **BIL (Business Interrruption Loss)**

  - **EDP Equipment:** The loss suffered from the inability to perform the computer's tasks for the time period required to replace the equipment. Do not consider the reduction in the loss that would occur from the performance of all or part of the computer's jobs by a clerical task force.

  - **Data:** The loss suffered from the non-availability of machine readable data for half the time period required to reconstruct all of the data files.

- **Program and Operating System:** The same type of loss as suffered for EDP Equipment for half the period required to complete all programs, plus the loss resulting from having clerical personnel working with simple listings of data until half of the programs have been completed.

- **Documentation:** The loss suffered as the result of delay in changing systems and programs for half the time period required to complete the recreation of the documentation.

d. Performance Failure Loss with Current Backup

For these columns, assume that the backup facility provides exactly the recovery capability it was intended to furnish. If backup for a given asset (e.g., data) does not exist, repeat the data from the "Without Backup" column.

- **ETR (Estimated Time to Recover)**

    - **EDP Equipment:** If an agreement has been made with another EDP installation for equipment backup, calculate based on the number of days it would take to become operational for half of the normal work load. If an agreement for EDP equipment backup for up to half of the normal work load has not been arranged, repeat the figure from the "Without Backup" column.

    - **Installation Facility:** Same calculation as the EDP Equipment figure above.

    - **Data, Programs, and Documentation:** If a satisfactory secondary (backup) storage site has been established to house these three assets, calculate on the number of days required to become fully operational for each of them. If a satisfactory secondary storage facility has not been established, repeat the figure from the "Without Backup" column for each of the items that is not protected.

- **EE (Extra Expense)**

    Given the existing backup capabilities, calculate the additional cost for each of the categories of assets that would be incurred until a full, normal operating condition has been achieved. Among the costs that might be incurred are the purchase of computer time, travel to and from other computer installations, cost of overtime of clerical personnel, the hiring of temporary workers, etc.

- **BIL (Business Interruption Loss)**

  Given the existing backup capabilities, calculate the financial loss incurred as the result of the inability to conduct normal business operations for the period required to achieve the normal operating level. An example would be the profit reduction resulting from the inability to meet production schedules due to the loss of a portion of the inventory status records.

e. **Performance Failure Loss with Desired Backup**

  For these columns, assume that the best possible backup capabilities are available and will function as intended. If no significant improvements can be seriously contemplated, repeat the data from the "Current Backup" columns.

  For the desired backup capabilities, use the same concepts and techniques in determining the Estimated Time to Recover, the Extra Expense, and Business Interruption Loss as were used for the "Current Backup" calculations. In filling out the Worksheet (Figure 11-2), Probable Economic Loss, use the space provided to identify briefly the desired backup capability with the associated One-Time Cost and Annual Continuing Cost. If no improvement in your backup facility is being considered, state "None Planned."

11.4 POSSIBLE COSTS OF SECURITY

At the same time that the probability of disruption is being considered and probable economic losses are being studied, ideas for security should be gathered and costs evaluated.

Some of the security items that could be considered are:

1. Backup Air Conditioning Unit

2. More Extensive Alarm System

3. Changes in Computer Room Construction

4. Closed Circuit TV Installation

5. Installation of Halogen Fire Extinguishing System

6. Extra Librarian in I/O Control

7. Extra Training of Personnel

8. Personnel to Produce Complete Documentation

9. Personnel to Work on Security Measures

10. Reprogramming Critical Programs for Better Control
    and Audit Trail.

11. More Frequent File Dumping

12. More Extensive Backup of Files

13. Uninterruptible Power Supply (U.P.S.)

14. Fire-Proof Vault

15. Full Personnel I.D. Card System

16. Extra Terminals, Supplied as Security Terminals

17. Securing Physical Communications Lines

18. Redundant Lines and Equipment

19. Cryptographic Techniques for Transmission, etc.

It is the responsibility of EDP management to select from this list and other ideas, then to create a priority list of items believed to be most effective. **Figure 11-3, Possible Costs of Security,** can be used for listing the desired security items with their cost. None will be 100% effective. Just as there should be an estimate of the probability of occurrence of loss, there should also be an estimate of the probable effectiveness of the security item. Once again, a simple rating should be used, such as:

1. High Effectiveness

2. Medium Effectiveness

3. Low Effectiveness

Security costs and effectiveness data derived from Figure 11-3 can be presented in order of importance for comparison in a Request For Expenditure. If a more sophisticated presentation is necessary, "Present Values" could be calculated. The numbers could also be related according to their probabilities of effectiveness.

In whatever way the information is finally presented, these worksheets will provide a valuable base for discussion of the problem. They define the dimensions of the problem and the importance of the considerations for management.

Figure 11-3

POSSIBLE COSTS OF SECURITY

(Dollars in Thousands)

No.	Security Item	One-Time Cost	Monthly Cost	Probable Effectiveness

Probable Effectiveness Codes:

1. High Effectiveness
2. Medium Effectiveness
3. Low Effectiveness

SECTION 12

INSURANCE AS A COVERAGE

SECTION OVERVIEW

Insurance does not prevent or detect security violations, but it can reduce the impact of loss. Insurance should be thought of as a control. It requires the same thorough evaluation as any other control. This section provides a series of worksheets to aid data processing management in making insurance decisions.

12.1   INSURANCE CONCERNS

The principle of insurance coverage is to transfer risk of major loss to another organization. Each company or organization will have its own standards as to what risk it will hold internally and what risk is to be transferred.

There will normally be an insurance manager, or equivalent, responsible for deciding the degree of risk to be insured. It is the responsibility of the data processing manager to present the problem to the insurance manager. He should first estimate the possible exposure. He should then outline in detail all the equipment, records, and media under his control, stating their replacement cost and actual cash value.

The need for this coverage, or any other special insurance coverage such as third party liability, business interruption, and so on, should be clearly defined. There may be, for example, a considerable business interruption loss which could be insured. This is normally not under the data processing manager's control, however. It should be reviewed and requested by the user management together with the insurance manager.

When data processing equipment is leased or rented, the insurance on it may be borne by the owner. This should be checked in the contract.

The insurance manager will also be concerned that all legal requirements for fire safety are being met in the facility. Insurance will only be valid if there is full compliance with all fire and safety laws. It is wise to request inspections by both the insurance company and the local fire department. Fire department familiarity with your installation is in itself a useful precaution. Contingency Plans are also useful.

The final decision on the insurance coverage will be determined by the organization policy on such matters. The decision can best be made if the data processing manager first:

- Develops a Contingency Plan

- Fills Out the Worksheets Carefully

- c.   Considers the Probabilities of Disaster

There will probably be three basic types of insurance policies to discuss:

- Fire Insurance

- Valuable Papers and Records Insurance

- All Risk Data Processing Insurance with Media and Records Section.

12.2   INSURANCE WORKSHEETS

Worksheets are provided in this Section to aid this process. These worksheets should be filled out by the data processing manager for discussion with the organization's insurance manager.

Figures 12-1-1 and 12-1-2: Insurance Coverage, Data Processing and Related Equipment Worksheets

These worksheets are used for listing all computers and peripheral equipment, as well as air conditioning and other component parts dedicated to the systems and data processing installation. Include shared facilities, such as air conditioning systems, only if the entire system is dedicated to the data processing installation. If it is shared as part of a central plant unit and insured accordingly, do not include it. Exclude furniture and fixtures unless they are unique to the EDP function and not apt to be covered under standard property policies. Report gross estimated amounts for the categories. For the purpose of this survey, detailed listings by piece of equipment are not required. However, they may be useful for the data processing manager's records.

Note the following definitions:

> **Replacement Cost** - The cost to replace the property in question with a modern unit, in new condition and of equivalent capacity, taking into consideration new materials, technology, and design concepts.

> **Actual Cash Value** - Replacement cost less an allowance for physical depreciation (not book depreciation) and functional or economic obsolescence.

Figure 12-2: Records and Media Worksheet

This worksheet is for listing all records and media used or stored in the data processing operation. This includes input records, magnetic media records, paper tape records, documentation, printed forms, and stored output.

It can be divided into:

a. **Active Data Processing Media** - All forms of converted data and programs written on vehicles actively employed in the system. This includes magnetic and perforated tapes, disks, drums, punch cards, etc.

b. **Source Material** - All records and data required for the preparation and updating of active processing media. This includes checks, statements, bills, invoices, credit ratings, accounting and service records, etc.

It is worth listing all types of records or media for insurance purposes. Media vary greatly in importance, however. There should be insurance to cover all media, but in varying amounts depending on importance or need. Media, with the information on them, may be classified as:

> **Vital** - Critical organization information that must be replaced with the records in event of disaster.

Important - Part of regular cyclical processing that may need reconstitution to proceed with the next cycle or to complete the audit trail.

Expendable - Useful information that may possibly be needed, but is far enough back in the cycle so it probably does not need reconstitution. Only the physical tape, disk, etc., will need replacing.

Figure 12-3: Extra Emergency Expense Worksheet

This worksheet is used for listing the additional cost required to continue the normal operations of the business immediately following damage to systems equipment, media, and necessary source material. Essentially, it is the excess of total operating cost during the restoration period over and above the total operating cost which would have been incurred if there had been no loss. Thus, the amount that the expenses will be reduced at the original location must be deducted.

List all emergency expenses that may be incurred in case of a major equipment breakdown, fire, or other disaster. A few of the possible expenses are listed on the sheet.

Figure 12-4: Third Party Liability Worksheet

This worksheet is applicable to any service bureau operation, or any systems work, that is provided by your Organization for outside customers. Special insurance coverage (errors and omissions) protects the insured against losses experienced by third parties through the insured's own negligence, error, or omission in providing data processing services.

Figure 12-5: Revenue Bearing Data Worksheet

This worksheet is used for listing records such as accounts receivable, fixed assets, etc., in active data processing media form which are the basis for future revenue claims. If applicable, it should also be used for identification and location of the Organization's assets that are leased to customers or used for other revenue bearing purposes. Loss or damage to such records generally constitutes exposure to losses greater than that of restoration costs or reconstruction.

Figure 12-6: Business Interruption Insurance Worksheet

The consideration of Business Interruption Insurance, or Loss of Profits Insurance, will depend on the individual circumstances of the data processing organization. If the main product is outside service, this insurance should be seriously considered and the calculation of it will be fairly straightforward. The organization will have income history and projections, and will have an idea of the effectiveness of emergency backup arrangements.

If the data processing organization is principally a service group within a larger organization, with no formal payments, the loss of profits must be considered for the larger organization in the event of an emergency. Discussions with the users will yield the type of coverage desired. As the users become aware of the problem of a possible emergency, there will probably be funds available to prepare for contingency operation.

Figure 12-7: Outside Computer Services Worksheet

Another insurance problem arises if the organization's data processing requirements are handled predominantly by outside computer services. The data processing media and data are in the control of a third party and there is an exposure to damage or loss that is not covered by the normal organization security measures.

This exposure must be estimated and discussed with the outside computer service. It is important to know if the service bureaus with whom you contract maintain errors and omissions coverage to protect you from loss of profits as a result of their failure, negligence, error or omission in providing services to you. They should also have normal insurance that covers loss or damage to any of your property in their custody.

Figure 12-1-1

INSURANCE COVERAGE

DATA PROCESSING AND RELATED EQUIPMENT

Owned Equipment

No.	Description	Date Installed	Replacement Cost	Actual Cash Value
1.	CPU			
2.	Peripheral Equipment			
3.	Terminals			
*4.				

*List other directly associated equipment

Insurance Coverage on Owned Equipment

Insurance Company	Date of Policy	Policy Amount	Annual Premium	Amount of Deductible

Briefly describe perils named or excluded in the above policies:

Figure 12-1-2

INSURANCE COVERAGE

DATA PROCESSING AND RELATED EQUIPMENT

Rented or Leased Equipment

No.	Contract/Lessor*	Date of Lease	Term of Lease	Annual Lease Cost	Lessor** Liability

*   If there are several contracts with a given lessor, these may be combined.

**   Indicate the extent to which the lessor assumes liability for equip-ment damage or loss, installed and in transit.

Insurance Coverage on Leased Equipment

Insurance Company	Date of Policy	Policy Amount	Annual Premium	Amount of Deductible

If you are covered separately for the difference in conditions if the rental/lease agreement is on a named peril basis and not on an all-risks peril basis, list the coverage.

Figure 12-2

INSURANCE COVERAGE

RECORDS AND MEDIA

No.	Number and Type of Records and Media	Need or Priority*	Retention Period	Cost to Reproduce	Replacement Value	Extra Expense

* 1. Vital   2. Important   3. Expendable

Insurance Coverage on Records and Media

Insurance Company	Date of Policy	Policy Amount	Annual Premium	Amount of Deductible

Note: If the above coverage includes the cost of reconstruction and research if either, or both, active media and source material were destroyed.

Figure 12-3

INSURANCE COVERAGE

EXTRA EMERGENCY EXPENSE

No.	Expense	Rate of Expense	Total Per Week	Total Per Month
1.	Rental of Temporary Facilities			
2.	Rental of Backup Equipment			
3.	Rental of Other Equipment			
4.	Rental of Furniture			
5.	Extra Supplies			
6.	Moving Costs			
7.	Temporary Insurance Costs			
8.	Extra Telephone Costs			
9.	Extra Traveling Costs			
10.	Overtime Payments to Employees			
11.	Additional Employees			
12.				
13.				
14.				
15.				
	DEDUCT			
	Expenses Reduced at Original Location			
	TOTAL Extra Expense:			

Insurance Coverage on Extra Emergency Expense

Insurance Company	Date of Policy	Policy Amount	Annual Premium	Amount of Deductible

Figure 12-4

INSURANCE COVERAGE

THIRD PARTY LIABILITY

NOTE: This worksheet is used only if any service bureau operations, or systems work, are provided by your organization for outside customers.

Total Sales of Computer Services to Customers: $_____

Total Sales of Systems Work to Customers: $_____

Insurance Coverage on Third Party Liability

Insurance Company	Date of Policy	Policy Amount	Annual Premium	Amount of Deductible

If you have reciprocal backup agreements with other organizations having similar equipment configurations, include in this list:

a. Coverage for losses incurred to your property by non-organization personnel.

b. Coverage for losses incurred to non-organizations' property by your personnel.

Figure 12-5

INSURANCE COVERAGE

REVENUE BEARING DATA

Indicate average outstanding balances for a one-year period for revenue bearing data in media form. Specify by type of data.

Average Outstanding Balance in 19_____

_____	$ _____
_____	$ _____
_____	$ _____
_____	$ _____

Insurance Coverage on Revenue Bearing Data

Insurance Company	Date of Policy	Policy Amount	Annual Premium	Amount of Deductible

Figure 12-6

INSURANCE COVERAGE

BUSINESS INTERRUPTION INSURANCE
(or Loss of Profits Insurance)

Is the coverage under:

a. Standard Fire Policy?   _____

b. Data Processing Insurance Policy?   _____

c. No Coverage   _____

Explain:

Insurance Coverage on Business Interruption

Insurance Company	Date of Policy	Policy Amount	Annual Premium	Amount of Deductible

Figure 12-7

INSURANCE COVERAGE

OUTSIDE COMPUTER SERVICES

NOTE: This worksheet is used only if your data processing requirements are handled predominantly by outside computer services.

1.   What is the extent of your exposure to damage or loss of data processing media in the possession of outside computer services? If none, explain.

2.   Do the service bureaus with whom you contract for services maintain errors and omissions coverage to protect you from loss of profits as a result of their failure, negligence, error, or omission in providing services to you?

   If this is in writing, attach a copy.

SECTION 13

RISK ANALYSIS

SECTION OVERVIEW

Risks are ever present in a computerized environment. They are generated by a variety of threats. Some of these threats are physical, such as fire, water damage, earthquake, hurricane. Other threats are people-oriented, such as errors, omissions, acts of violence, fraud, theft. These risks cannot be eliminated, but security measures can reduce the probability of the risk turning into a damaging event.

Part of any security evaluation should be an assessment of the security risks and their magnitude. This need not be a time-consuming process, but it is an essential part of preparing for the evaluation. The remainder of the evaluation is an assessment of the adequacy of the security measures to deal with those risks. The risks can be to the environment or to the application.

This section provides two approaches to assessing risks. These are:

a. **Data Processing Organizational Risks,** using a risk-probing checklist to identify the characteristics of the environment that lead to good computer security.

b. <u>Computer Operations Risks,</u> using a checklist of risks common to computerized installations.

13.1   RISK ANALYSIS IN A SECURITY EVALUATION

Risk analysis is a systematic comparison of the risks to an organization's resources, the personnel, application, and computer system vulnerabilities, and the existing controls against the risks. A risk analysis can be handled in three ways:

- **Subjectively defined** by management, posssibly because of over-riding legal considerations, such as the Foreign Corrupt Practices Act.

- **Scored by estimating procedures,** this technique is discussed in detail in Volume II of the FTP Technical Library manual "EDP Security," to give a yardstick for management to consider.

- **Estimated with detailed calculations,** as proposed by the National Bureau of Standards. This approach is outlined in detail in the FTP Technical Library manual, "EDP Disaster Recovery".

Any approach to risk analysis essentially combines the loss exposure for each resource, or combination of resources, with an estimated rate of occurrence to establish a potential level of damage to assets or resources. This gives an estimate in terms of dollars which can be compared to the cost of protection and control measures. A decision can then be made as to which measures to put in place, and management will have a good estimate of their exposures.

Risk analysis attempts to identify all the potential risks facing the operation, and to estimate the possible severity of the risks. A risk is the potential for loss or damage to an organization from materialized threats. A threat is a possible damaging event that can occur. If a threat occurs, it exploits a vulnerability in the security of a computer-based organization.   The risk can be measured to a large extent by performing a risk analysis process.

The security reviewer should, therefore, evaluate a computerized environment's vulnerability to the materialization of risk. Vulnerability is a weakness in an organization that may be exploited by a threat to cause destruction or misuse of its assets or resources. In examining these vulnerabilities, the reviewer also assesses the strength of the controls that reduce the risk, or vulnerability to risk, to an acceptable level.

The objective of a security risk analysis process is to estimate the exposure resulting from a risk. The reviewer must estimate the exposure before dealing with the risk as a security problem. Good security practice dictates that an organization should not spend more to reduce an exposure than the potential loss that might result from that exposure, unless other legal requirements take precedence.

From the point of view of a security reviewer of an EDP operation, consideration of all the tasks in the risk management program is essential for using the tool to its best advantage.

13.2   STEPS IN RISK ASSESSMENT

The detail involved and the calculations to be made for a risk analysis will vary greatly, depending on the way a risk assessment is handled: subjective decision, scoring procedures, or detailed calculations, as discussed. In any of these approaches, however, the order of consideration of the factors involved should be the same ten steps. These steps are as follows:

Step 1 - Preliminary Considerations

Solicit top management commitment to the review process and delegate responsibility to a team for the risk assessment program.

Step 2 - Asset Identification

Identify resources, including hardware, software, data, personnel, supplies, communications, facilities, etc.

Step 3 - Asset Valuation

Determine the sensitivity and value of assets to the owner, and a possible abuser.

Step 4 - Vulnerability Analysis

Identify weaknesses within the organization, particularly in its computer systems.

Step 5 - Threat Analysis

Identify external menaces or abusive forces that can destroy or misuse the resources.

Step 6 - Threat/Vulnerability Paring

Determine how the threats can combine with the vulnerabilities to cause loss or damage.

Step 7 - Loss Exposure Value

Use a methodology where loss exposure is calculated or estimated for each threat/vulnerability attacking an asset.

Step 8 - Predictive Analysis

Identify frequency of the threat/vulnerability materialization with respect to an asset. This is the frequency of loss exposure.

Step 9 - Exposure (Risk) Assessment

Use a method for evaluating loss exposure frequency and loss exposure values to obtain some estimate of the value or severity for each damaging event, and then for all possible damaging events. This process will result in an estimated severity or value for each risk.

Step 10 - Decision On The Probable Risk Involved

Assess the reasonableness of the calculations for combinations of the risks and safeguards. Prepare a combination of safeguards comprising a system of security based on the findings, and present to management.

13.3 METHODS OF RISK IDENTIFICATION

To perform a risk assessment for a security review, it is necessary for the reviewer to identify the possible security risks and threats. This occurs in Steps 4, 5, and 6 of the Risk Assessment outlined above. There are a variety of ways to identify security risks and threats. Two environmental risk identifications are recommended for small computer centers. They are:

- Data Processing Organization Risks
- Computer Operations Security Risks

For some applications, risk scoring methods may be appropriate. These techniques are treated in detail in the FTP Technical Library manual, "EDP Security."

Management checklists list a number of vulnerabilities grouped according to common system organizational structures. These lists are not intended to be all-inclusive, but are to suggest the various types of vulnerabilities that may exist in different systems. This is only a preliminary identification and analysis to determine the amount of effort that should be put into the security review, and the amount of management attention that is deserved.

- **Data Processing Environmental or Organizational Risks**

  This subjective method uses checklists to identify the characteristics of the environment that correlate to good computer security, and the security measures that should be in place.

- **Computer Operations Security Risks**

  These checklists help the reviewers get an overview of the environment in which the application systems operate, to make them aware of the many undesirable events which can have serious consequences.

These methods are used to identify the risks in Steps 4 through 6, above. After they have been used, Steps 7 through 9 require the reviewers to evaluate the severity of each risk. This can be accomplished as simply as applying a three-level judgment as follows:

A = High Risk
B = Average Risk
C = Low Risk

99

After which, management would consider the threats and the reasonable response to them. On the other hand, this evaluation can be as complex as the process recommended by the National Bureau of Standards (see Volume I, Section 8 of the FTP Technical Library manual "EDP Security"). In this process, an annual dollar loss is calculated for each item of value in the organization. These dollar values are used to determine whether security safeguards are required, and the cost that can be allocated for the safeguard.

Risk analysis techniques should yield a quantitative statement of the effect of specific risks. A statement of the probability of the occurrence of a particular event is essential to a useful risk assessment. There are two key elements in risk analysis. These are:

- A statement of impact that is, the damage caused by a specific difficulty.

- A statement of the probability of encountering that difficulty within a specified period of time.

Both parameters are needed to describe risk in terms of cost per unit time, such as dollars per year.

The probability of an undesirable thing happening is usually more difficult to determine with confidence than is a measure of the impact of its happening. It has been suggested that we are so accustomed to making subjective judgments of probability in reaching decisions that it is difficult to accept a formalization of the process. However, statements of the potential economic impacts of events without regard to their relative probability cannot lead to the identification of those security exposures that are worthy of corrective action. Probability of occurrence is also a significant factor. There are many events which could have catastrophic consequences but have such a low probability of occurrence as to not justify protective measures.

13.4   IDENTIFICATION OF ENVIRONMENTAL RISKS

The security environment established by management has a significant impact on the selection of a company's security procedures and techniques and general effectiveness.

The security environment is shaped by several factors. Some are clearly visible, like a formal corporate security policy statement which is followed. Some are intangible, like the competence and integrity of personnel. Some, like organizational structure and the way in which management communicates, enforces, and reinforces policy, vary so widely among companies that they can be contrasted more easily than they can be compared.

It is difficult to measure the significance of each factor, but it is generally possible to make an overall evaluation. An overall evaluation of a company's environment is a necessary prelude to the evaluation of its security control procedures and techniques.

A weak security environment would make some security measures ineffective. For example, individuals in an organization may hesitate to challenge a management override of a specific security procedure. It is possible for security procedures and techniques to work in a company that has a poor security environment. However, it is unlikely that management can have reasonable assurance that the broad objectives of security are being met, unless the company has an environment that establishes an appropriate level of security consciousness.

The security environment established by management sets the tone of security for the organization. This section provides a checklist of probing security questions. "No" answers are only **indicative** of potential security problems and should be investigated further in the security review.

Figure 13-1, Identification of Environmental Risks, points up a number of areas which could possibly indicate weak points in the operation and control of the computers. It is divided into five parts:

A. Security Atmosphere

B. Authorization

C. Recording of Information

D. Asset Safeguarding

E. Accountability

Figure 13-1
(Page 1)

IDENTIFICATION OF ENVIRONMENTAL RISKS

No.	Item	Yes	No	N/A	Comments
	A. Security Atmosphere				
1.	Does a formal security policy exist?				
2.	Is the structure of the organization representative of the way things actually happen in the organization?				
3.	Does management receive regular reports on violations of security?				
4.	Do violations of the organization's security policies and procedures receive prompt attention?				
5.	Are the expenditures of the organization controlled by a budgetary procedure?				
6.	Are senior members of management concerned with the adequacy of security in their area of responsibility in the organization?				
7.	Is there an internal audit department?				
8.	Does the internal audit department report directly or indirectly to the audit committee and/or a senior member of management outside the financial area?				
9.	Are audit findings and recommendations, from both internal and external auditors, promptly acted upon?				
10.	Does the organization punish and/or prosecute employees found guilty of fraud and embezzlement of organization assets?				
11.	Does a formal policy exist stating who is responsible for authorizing each type of transaction?				
12.	Has the organization established formal policies regarding improper use of corporate funds as defined in the Foreign Corrupt Practices Act?				
13.	Does the organization have an open-door policy which permits employees to visit any member of management to discuss employee problems and/or grievances?				

Figure 13-1
(Page 2)

IDENTIFICATION OF ENVIRONMENTAL RISKS

No.	Item	Responses			
		Yes	No	N/A	Comments
	A. Security Atmosphere (Continued)				
14.	Do either auditors or a quality assurance group independently assess the adequacy of security in computerized applications?				
15.	Do senior officers of the organization receive, review, and act upon security complaints?				
	B. Authorization				
16.	Are there specific authorization policies and/or procedures that outline management's specific authorization to access assets?				
17.	Are annual operating plans approved by senior management?				
18.	Are annual operating budgets approved by senior management?				
19.	Are job descriptions established for each position in the organization?				
20.	Do job descriptions establish and limit the amount of authority for each position?				
21.	Are organizational charts approved by senior management?				
22.	Are salary procedures established and followed?				
23.	Are hiring practices established and followed?				
24.	Is there a controller's manual outlining the financial policies and procedures?				
25.	Are individuals' authorities limited by a specific dollar limit?				

103

Figure 13-1
(Page 3)

IDENTIFICATION OF ENVIRONMENTAL RISKS

No.	Item	Yes	No	N/A	Comments
	B. Authorization (Continued)				
26.	Are employees informed as to the types of commitments they can and cannot make in the name of their organization?				
27.	Are all contracts reviewed by legal counsel?				
28.	Are production/conversion plans and schedules approved?				
29.	Do the By-Laws of the corporation spell out authorization for the purchase and sale of capital assets, securities, and contracts?				
30.	Are the methods of implementing generally accepted accounting principles approved?				
	C. Recording of Information				
31.	Does a complete chart of accounts exist?				
32.	Is each account adequately described to indicate the type of transactions that should be recorded using that account number?				
33.	Are procedures established to determine that transactions are recorded in the appropriate accounting period?				
34.	Are transactions recorded in accordance with generally accepted accounting procedures?				
35.	Is sufficient data recorded with each transaction so that the processing that occurred in creating the transaction can be reconstructed if necessary?				
36.	Are all negotiable instruments prenumbered?				
37.	Are key documents such as purchase orders, invoices, etc., prenumbered?				

Figure 13-1
(Page 4)

IDENTIFICATION OF ENVIRONMENTAL RISKS

No.	Item	Responses			
		Yes	No	N/A	Comments
	C. Recording of Information (Continued)				
38.	Is appropriate control maintained over pre-numbered documents so that the loss of one or more documents would be recognized and investigated?				
39.	Are controls sufficent to ensure that only actual transactions are recorded?				
40.	Are controls sufficient to ensure that the recorded amounts are correct?				
41.	Are controls sufficient to ensure that all recorded transactions are included in the financial statements?				
42.	Are procedures developed to ensure that the recording of transactions is independent from the authority to initiate or authorize those transactions?				
43.	Are procedures developed to ensure that the record-keeping function is organizationally independent of the function having responsibility for the custody of assets?				
44.	Are procedures developed to ensure that all changes, adjustments, corrections, and alterations to recorded amounts are recorded on a timely basis?				
45.	Are procedures established so that all recorded transactions are properly classified?				
46.	Are procedures established so that all recorded transactions are properly summarized?				
47.	Are procedures established to ensure that recorded transactions will be retained in accordance with the organization's retention procedures and government regulations?				

Figure 13-1
(Page 5)

IDENTIFICATION OF ENVIRONMENTAL RISKS

No.	Item	Yes	No	N/A	Comments
	D. Asset Safeguarding				
48.	Are important records protected against physical hazards?				
49.	Is access restricted to offices, plants, etc., according to the value of the assets in those premises?				
50.	Are securities and cash, except those needed for the day-to-day operation of the business, in vaults or equally safe areas?				
51.	Are supplies of unused negotiable instruments stored in a safe place under the custody of a senior member of management?				
52.	Are facsimile signature plates stored in a safe place under the custody of a senior member of management?				
53.	Are unusable or spoiled negotiable instruments voided, and the voided document stored in a secure area until destroyed?				
54.	Is accountability for inventory assigned to a specific individual?				
55.	Is the adequacy of protection over inventory stored at outside locations, such as public warehouses, investigated prior to storing inventory in those locations?				
56.	Do procedures exist for the timely reporting of losses of assets?				
57.	Do procedures exist for the involvement of security, audit, and/or law enforcement agencies to investigate losses?				
58.	Are losses covered by insurance reported to the insurance companies on a timely basis?				
59.	Are procedures established to physically destroy (e.g. shredding or burning) confidential documents?				

Figure 13-1
(Page 6)

IDENTIFICATION OF ENVIRONMENTAL RISKS

No.	Item	Yes	No	N/A	Comments
	D. Asset Safeguarding (Continued)				
60.	Do procedures exist that require employees to be instructed in the performance of their job tasks?				
61.	Are job functions adequately documented so that the organization is not dependent upon the continued employment of any single employee?				
62.	Are computerized business applications adequately documented so that the organization is not dependent upon the continued employment of any single employee?				
63.	Have alternate sources of supply been established in the event that one source of supply should become unavailable?				
64.	Are procedures established regarding the entry and movement of visitors through the organization's premises?				
65.	Are procedures established regarding the removal from the organization's premises of any policies, procedures, manuals, correspondence, documentation, or other assets for use by that employee at premises other than those of the organization?				
66.	Are procedures established regarding employees giving talks, writing articles, books, etc., about company products, procedures, and operations?				
67.	Have procedures been established to safeguard employees while on the premises?				
68.	Are procedures established to classify the organization's information according to its importance to the organization?				
69.	Has the privacy of information about individuals been adequately protected?				

Figure 13-1
(Page 7)

IDENTIFICATION OF ENVIRONMENTAL RISKS

No.	Item	Yes	No	N/A	Comments
	D. Asset Safeguarding (Continued)				
70.	Have adequate procedures been made to fight disasters, such as fire, flood, etc., should they occur?				
71.	Have alarm devices been installed to protect critical areas against intrusion and/or disasters such as fire?				
72.	Have procedures been established to protect the organization's information from unauthorized access through communication lines?				
73.	Have procedures been established to safeguard the organization's computerized information?				
	E. Accountability				
74.	Is there an independent audit function established to compare the recorded accountability for assets with the existing assets?				
75.	Does internal audit make the comparison of recorded accountability for assets with the existing assets at reasonable intervals?				
76.	Are individual assets identified, and is that identification recorded?				
77.	Is the physical location of all assets recorded?				
78.	Do procedures establish a specified time period in which appropriate action must be taken with respect to any differences between recorded accountability for assets and the existence of those assets?				
79.	Are the consequences under the Foreign Corrupt Practices Act arising from differences between recorded accountability for assets with the existing assets evaluated and appropriate action taken?				

Figure 13-1
(Page 8)

IDENTIFICATION OF ENVIRONMENTAL RISKS

No.	Item	Yes	No	N/A	Comments
	E. Accountability (Continued)				
80.	Do procedures specify the methods for this comparison, such as counts of physical inventory observed by auditors, confirmation of accounts receivable, etc.?				
81.	Is a single individual made accountable for each asset?				
82.	Are procedures established so that the individual will verify the existence of assets at regular intervals?				

13.5   IDENTIFICATION OF COMPUTER OPERATIONS SECURITY RISKS

The reviewer must evaluate the effectiveness of existing security controls in the operations area to determine the risks present in the computerized environment. After the risks are understood, and the effectiveness of controls and security measures are evaluated, in general, the reviewer can estimate the effort to make a detailed review of all security aspects of the computer operation.

A summarized list of risks is provided in **Figure 13-2, Common Computer Operations Security Risks,** to help explain and uncover the possible risks in a computerized environment. This checklist is given as a tool for the reviewer to use to identify what particular areas should be examined in the computer area in a security review.

The checklist should be filled out by a knowledgeable team of operations and security personnel to determine which of the risks listed may be applicable to the area under review. The team could then make their estimate of whether a more detailed security review is called for, or whether the in-place security measures are probably sufficient to control those risks. Many of the questions may not be aplicable to a particular installation. If the questions are not pertinent, they should be checked in the N/A column.

Figure 13-2
(Page 1)

COMMON COMPUTER OPERATIONS SECURITY RISKS

No.	Item	Yes	No	N/A	Comments
	A. Erroneous or Falsified Data Input				
1.	Unreasonable or inconsistent source data values may not be detected.				
2.	Keying errors during transcription may not be detected.				
3.	Incomplete or poorly formatted data records may be accepted and treated as if they were complete records.				
4.	Records in one format may be interpreted according to a different format.				
5.	An employee may fraudulently add, delete, or modify data (e.g. payment vouchers, claims) to obtain benefits (e.g. checks, negotiable coupons).				
6.	Lack of document counts and other controls over source data or input transactions may allow some of the data or transactions to be lost without detection, or allow extra records to be added.				
7.	Records about the data entry personnel (e.g., a record of a personnel action) may be modified during data entry.				
8.	Data which arrives at the last minute (or under some other special or emergency condition) may not be verified prior to processing.				
9.	Records in which errors have been detected may be corrected without verification of the full record.				
	B. Misuse by Authorized End Users				
10.	An employee may convert information to an unauthorized use; for example, he may sell privileged data about an individual to a prospective employer, credit agency, insurance company, or competitor; or he may use information for stock market transactions before their public release.				

111

Figure 13-2
(Page 2)

COMMON COMPUTER OPERATIONS SECURITY RISKS

No.	Item	Responses			
		Yes	No	N/A	Comments
	B. Misuse by Authorized End Users (Continued)				
11.	A user whose job requires access to individual records in a file may manage to compile a complete listing of the file and then make unauthorized use of it (e.g. sell a listing of employees' home addresses as a mailing list).				
12.	Unauthorized altering of information may be accomplished for an unauthorized end user (e.g. theft of services).				
13.	An authorized user may use the computer system for personal benefit (e.g., theft of services).				
14.	A supervisor may manage to approve and enter a fraudulent transaction.				
15.	A disgruntled or terminated employee may destroy or modify records, possibly in such a way that backup records are also corrupted and useless.				
16.	An authorized user may accept a bribe to modify or obtain information.				
	C. Uncontrolled System Access				
17.	Data or programs may be stolen from the computer room, or other storage areas.				
18.	EDP facilities may be destroyed or damaged by either intruders or employees.				
19.	Individuals may not be adequately identified before they are allowed to enter the EDP area.				
20.	Remote terminals may not be adequately protected from use by unauthorized persons.				
21.	An unauthorized user may gain access to the system via a dial-in line and an authorized user's password.				

Figure 13-2
(Page 3)

COMMON COMPUTER OPERATIONS SECURITY RISKS

No.	Item	Responses			
		Yes	No	N/A	Comments
	C. Uncontrolled System Access (Continued)				
22.	Passwords may be inadvertently revealed to unauthorized individuals. A user may write his password in some convenient place, or the password may be obtained from card decks, discarded printouts, or by observing the user as he types it.				
23.	A user may leave a logged-in terminal unattended, allowing an unauthorized person to use it.				
24.	A terminated employee may retain access to an EDP system because his name and password are not immediately deleted from authorization tables and control lists.				
25.	An unauthorized individual may gain access to the system for his own purposes (e.g. theft of computer services or data or programs, modification of data, alteration of programs, sabotage, denial of services).				
26.	Repeated attempts by the same user or terminal to gain unauthorized access to the system or to a file may go undetected.				
	D. Ineffective Security Practices for the Application				
27.	Poorly defined criteria for authorized access may result in employees not knowing what information they, or others, are permitted to access.				
28.	The person responsible for security may fail to restrict user access to only those processes and data which are needed to accomplish assigned tasks.				
29.	Large fund disbursements, unusual price changes, and unanticipated inventory usage may not be reviewed for correctness.				
30.	Repeated payments to the same party may go unnoticed because there is no review.				

Figure 13-2
(Page 4)

COMMON COMPUTER OPERATIONS SECURITY RISKS

No.	Item	Responses			
		Yes	No	N/A	Comments
	D. Ineffective Security Practices for the Application (Continued)				
31.	Sensitive data may be carelessly handled by the application staff, by the mail service, or by other personnel within the organization.				
32.	Postprocessing reports analyzing system operations may not be reviewed to detect security violations.				
33.	Inadvertent modification or destruction of files may occur when trainees are allowed to work on live data.				
34.	Appropriate action may not be pursued when a security variance is reported to the system security administration or to the perpetrating individual's supervisor. Procedures covering such occurrences may not exist.				
	E. Procedural and Control Errors in Computer Operation				
35.	Files may be destroyed during database reorganization or during release of disk space.				
36.	Operators may ignore operational procedures (e.g., by allowing programmers to operate computer equipment).				
37.	Job control language parameters may be erroneous.				
38.	An installation manager may circumvent operational controls to obtain information.				
39.	Careless or incorrect restarting after shutdown may cause the state of a transaction update to be unknown.				
40.	An operator may enter erroneous information at the CPU console (e.g. control switch in wrong position, terminal user allowed full system access, operator cancels wrong job from queue).				

Figure 13-2
(Page 5)

COMMON COMPUTER OPERATIONS SECURITY RISKS

No.	Item	Yes	No	N/A	Comments
	E. Procedural and Control Errors in Computer Operation (Continued)				
41.	Hardware maintenance may be performed while production data is on-line and the equipment undergoing maintenance is not isolated.				
42.	An operator may perform unauthorized acts for personal gain (e.g., make extra copies of competitive bidding reports, print copies of un-employment checks, delate a record from journal file).				
43.	Operations staff may sabotage the computer (e.g., break corrections or enter erroneous information).				
44.	The wrong version of a program may be executed.				
45.	A program may be executed twice using the same transactions.				
46.	An operator may bypass required safety controls.				
47.	Supervision of operations personnel may not be adequate during night shifts.				
48.	Due to incorrectly learned procedures, an operator may alter or erase the master files.				
49.	A console operator may override a label check without recording the action in the security log.				
	F. Storage Media Handling				
50.	Critical tape files may be mounted without being write protected.				
51.	Inadvertently or intentionally mislabeled storage media may be erased. In a case where they contain backup files, the erasure may not be noticed until it is needed.				

Figure 13-2
(Page 6)

COMMON COMPUTER OPERATIONS SECURITY RISKS

No.	Item	Yes	No	N/A	Comments
	F. Storage Media Handling (Continued)				
52.	Internal labels on storage media may not be checked for correctness.				
53.	Files with missing or mislabeled expiration dates may be erased.				
54.	Incorrect processing of data or erroneous updating of files may occur when card decks have been dropped, partial input decks are used, write rings mistakenly are placed in tapes, paper tape is incorrectly mounted, or wrong tape is mounted.				
55.	Scratch tapes used for jobs processing sensitive data may not be adequately erased after use.				
56.	Temporary files written during a job step for use in subsequent steps may be erroneously released or modified through inadequate protection of the files, or because of an abnormal termination.				
57.	Storage media containing sensitive information may not get adequate protection because operations staff is not advised of the nature of the information content.				
58.	Tape management procedures may not adequately account for the current status of all tapes.				
59.	Magnetic storage media that have contained very sensitive information may not be degaussed before being released.				
60.	Output may be sent to the wrong individual or terminal.				
61.	Improperly operating output or postprocessing units (e.g., bursters, decollators or multipart forms) may result in loss of output.				
62.	Surplus output material (e.g., dulpicates of output data, used carbon paper) may not be disposed of properly.				

Figure 13-2
(Page 7)

COMMON COMPUTER OPERATIONS SECURITY RISKS

No.	Item	Yes	No	N/A	Comments
63.	Tapes and programs that label output for distribution may be erroneous, or not protected from tampering.				
	G. Program Errors				
64.	Records may be deleted from sensitive files without a guarantee that the deleted records can be reconstructed.				
65.	Programmers may insert special provisions in programs that manipulate data concerning themselves (e.g., payroll programmer may alter his own payroll records).				
66.	Data may not be stored separately from code with the result that program modifications are more difficult and must be made more frequently.				
67.	Program changes may not be tested adequately before being used in a production run.				
68.	Changes to a program may result in new errors because of unanticipated interactions between program modules.				
69.	Program acceptance tests may fail to detect errors that only occur for unusual combinations of input (e.g., a program that is supposed to reject all except a specified range of values actually accepts an additional value).				
70.	Programs, the content of which should be safeguarded, may not be identified and protected.				
71.	Code, test data with its associated output, and documentation for certified programs may not be filed and retained for reference.				
72.	Documentation for vital programs may not be safeguarded.				

Figure 13-2
(Page 8)

COMMON COMPUTER OPERATIONS SECURITY RISKS

No.	Item	Yes	No	N/A	Comments
	G. Program Errors (Continued)				
73.	Programmers may fail to keep a change log, to maintain back copies, or to formalize record keeping activities.				
74.	An employee may steal programs he is maintaining and use them for personal gain (e.g., sale to a commercial organization).				
75.	Poor program design may result in a critical data value being initialized twice. An error may occur when the program is modified to change the data value, but only changes it in one place.				
76.	Production data may be disclosed or destroyed when it is used during testing.				
77.	Errors may result when the programmer misunderstands requests for changes to the program.				
78.	Errors may be introduced by a programmer who makes changes directly to machine code.				
79.	Programs may contain routines not compatible with their intended purpose, which can disable or bypass security protection mechanisms (e.g., a programmer who anticipates being fired inserts code into a program which will cause vital system files to be deleted as soon as his name no longer appears in the payroll file).				
80.	Inadequate documentation or labeling may result in wrong version of program being modified.				
	H. Operating System Flaws				
81.	User jobs may be permitted to read or write outside assigned storage area.				
82.	Inconsistencies may be introduced into data because of simultaneous processing of the same file by two jobs.				

Figure 13-2
(Page 9)

COMMON COMPUTER OPERATIONS SECURITY RISKS

No.	Item	Responses			
		Yes	No	N/A	Comments
	H. Operating System Flaws (Continued)				
83.	An operating system design or implementation error may allow a user to disable audit controls or to access all system information.				
84.	An operating system may not protect a copy of information as thoroughly as it protects the original.				
85.	Unauthorized modification to the operating system may allow a data entry clerk to enter programs and thus subvert the system.				
86.	An operating system crash may expose valuable information, such as password lists or authorization tables.				
87.	Maintenance personnel may bypass security controls while performing maintenance work. At such times the system is vulnerable to errors or intentional acts of the maintenance personnel, or anyone else who might also be on the system and discover the opening (e.g., microcoded sections of the operating system may be tampered with or sensitive information from on-line files may be disclosed).				
88.	An operating system may fail to record that multiple copies of output have been made from spooled storage devices.				
89.	An operating system may fail to maintain an unbroken audit trail.				
90.	When restarting after a system crash, the operating system may fail to ascertain that all terminal locations which were previously occupied are still occupied by the same individuals.				
91.	A user may be able to get into monitor or supervisory mode.				

Figure 13-2
(Page 10)

COMMON COMPUTER OPERATIONS SECURITY RISKS

No.	Item	Responses			
		Yes	No	N/A	Comments
92.	The operating system may fail to erase all scratch space assigned to a job after the normal or abnormal termination of the job.				
93.	Files may be allowed to be read or written without having been opened.				
	I. Communications System Failure				
94.	Undetected Accidental Failures:				
	a. Undetected communications errors may result in incorrect or modified data.				
	b. Information may be accidentally misdirected to the wrong terminal.				
	c. Communication nodes may leave unprotected fragments of messages in memory during unanticipated interruptions in processing.				
	d. Communication protocol may fail to positively identify the transmitter or receiver of a message.				
95.	Intentional Acts:				
	a. Communications lines may be monitored by unauthorized individuals.				
	b. Data or programs may be stolen via telephone circuits from a remote job entry terminal.				
	c. Programs in the network switching computers may be modified to compromise security.				
	d. Data may be deliberately changed by individuals tapping the line (requires some sophistication, but is applicable to financial data).				
	e. An unauthorized user may "take over" a computer communication port as an authorized user disconnects from it. Many systems cannot detect the change in much of the currently available communication protocols.				

Figure 13-2
(Page 11)

COMMON COMPUTER OPERATIONS SECURITY RISKS

No.	Item	Responses			
		Yes	No	N/A	Comments
	I. Communications System Failure				
	Intentional Acts (Continued):				
	f. If encryption is used, keys may be stolen.				
	g. A terminal user may be "spoofed" into providing sensitive data. system.				
	h. False messages may be inserted into the system.				
	i. True messages may be deleted from the system.				
	j. Messages may be recorded and replayed into the system (e.g., "Deposit $100" message).				

SECTION 14

DISASTER RECOVERY AND CONTINGENCY PLANS

SECTION OVERVIEW

Disaster recovery planning and arrangements for contingency backup operation are extremely important. This section provides information and procedures for planning a disaster recovery review and for developing the required contingency plans. A checklist is provided to aid in the analysis of the priority of concerns to management.

A useful approach is given to relating the cost of different levels of security and disaster recovery measures to need. Mandatory, necessary, and desirable measures are discussed as a relative scale for initial management analysis. Representative types of disaster are mentioned. The most probable disaster occurrences and key disaster scenarios are identified.

The planning for the preparation of an EDP Disaster Recovery Plan is described, including lists of the types of information to be derived. Identification of staff members who should participate in the creation and review of the plan is also discussed.

An EDP disaster recovery project plan (the plan for creating the plan) is described, and information requirements that are normal in the different areas of an EDP organization are specified. The need for management, user, and vendor agreements is discussed.

An example of an EDP Disaster Recovery Plan for a small computer system is outlined and described in three phases: 1) initial response; 2) disaster recovery at the backup site; and 3) recovery at the original site. It is recommended that a brief, written manual covering the EDP Disaster Recovery Procedures be prepared, distributed, and maintained.

An outline of a typical final report of a disaster recovery planning study is provided, with the recommendations for action to be presented to management.

14.1   MANAGEMENT REQUIREMENTS AND CONSIDERATIONS

The purpose of EDP disaster recovery planning is to prepare in advance to ensure the continuity of businesss information if the EDP capability is lost. Thus, disaster recovery planning, particularly as it is being planned and started, is a management rather than a technical issue. It deals with the realities of people, organizational relationships, and special interests. Disaster recovery actions are highly prioritized, and many normal operations are neglected. Management must take the lead and continually assess the technical considerations involved as to their utility.

Disaster recovery planning and arrangements for contingency backup operation are just as important, relatively, for small computer systems as they are for the larger systems. This section should be adequate for planning a disaster recovery review and developing the required contingency plans. If more information on the subject is desired, the best reference is the **FTP Technical Library publication, "EDP Disaster Recovery: Planning and Procedures."** Volume I covers the planning process. Volume II presents some typical procedures.

Management must realize that EDP professionals agree there are no entirely secure computers. Many computer operations have fine methods for security in place, and management can be assured that the best possible actions have been taken; but there are always people, electronics, and natural disasters that can suddenly disrupt the operations. Management must realistically look at:

a.   Legal Obligation Requirements

b.   Cash Flow Maintenance

c.   Customer Services

d.   Competitive Advantages

e.   Production and Distribution Decisions

f.   Logistics and Operations Control

g.   Purchasing Functions and Vendor Relationships

h.   Ongoing Project Control

i.   Branch or Agency Communications

j.   Personnel and Union Relations

k.   Shareholder and Public Relations

Management must assess the importance of the small computer system operations to these facets of their business, then decide the type of effort that should be put into the backup of the computer function.

- ### Priority Concerns of Management

The principal area of concern in disaster recovery operations for most organizations is the safety and well-being of the personnel involved. This concern should remain paramount. The principal business concern is the maintenance of accounting records and customer services. The business interruption loss must be kept as low as possible, and the required cash flow maintained. Legal and reporting requirements must, of course, be maintained also.

An additional fundamental concern is the protection of facilities, equipment, programs, and supplies. **Figure 14-1, Priority Concerns of Management,** is a checklist which expands on these concerns. Management can use it to check the fundamental, minimum requirements of a disaster recovery plan.

14.2   LEVELS OF SECURITY AND DISASTER RECOVERY MEASURES

A Disaster Recovery Plan is developed to minimize the costs resulting from losses of, or damages to, the resources or the capabilities of a computer facility and related services. It is dependent for success on the recognition of the potential consequences of undesirable happenings. There are many resources related to small computer system operations. Some particular subset of these is required to support each function that is provided to others in the organization. These resources include: people, programs, data, hardware, communications equipment and systems, electric power, the physical facility and access to it, and even items such as paper forms.

All resources are not equally important, nor are they equally susceptible to harm. The selection of safeguards and the elements of a contingency plan should, therefore, be done with an informed awareness of which system functions are supported by each resource element, and of the susceptibility of each element to harm. The cost-effective protection of a small computer system operation is thus dependent on:

- the importance to the organization of each of the component parts of the computer functions;

- the general probability of something undesirable happening to any of the components;

- the likely results and ramifications of various types of disasters that could occur;

- preparations that can be made to minimize the chances of disasters, and the costs if they do occur.

Any part of a Disaster Recovery Plan is overhead cost until it becomes necessary to activate it. It is, therefore, necessary to consider the importance of the resources and services, and to justify all the parts of security and disaster recovery measures by estimating the losses that could occur through lack of these precautions. The combination of initial expenditures and insurance coverage must be balanced against the necessity of the service and the probability of the need of the recovery procedures. There are some actions that are mandatory, however. They must be taken, whatever the cost.

Figure 14-1
(Page 1)

PRIORITY CONCERNS OF MANAGEMENT

No.	Item	Yes	No	N/A	Comments
	Staff Protection and Actions				
1.	Have all staff been trained in the fire alarm, bomb threat, and other emergency procedures?				
2.	Do all staff understand that when the alarm sounds they: a. immediately vacate the building? b. do not return to pick up items from desks? c. report to supervisors at designated points?				
3.	Do all staff know who to call in times of emergency or where the emergency telephone list is located?				
4.	Do the disaster recovery planning teams understand that the protection and safety of people in the area is paramount?				
5.	Have good management notification procedures been developed for any emergency of any size?				
	Maintenance of Customer Services and Cash Flow				
6.	Has management strictly prioritized the most necessary services to be maintained in an emergency?				
7.	Are all user groups involved in customer services and cash handling working with the plan teams?				
8.	For on-line customer services, can alternate operations be brought up within 24 hours?				
9.	Are most cash deposits sent directly to banks and not vulnerable to a disaster in the computer area?				
10.	Does the organization have plans for controlled public press releases in times of disaster?				

Figure 14-1
(Page 2)

PRIORITY CONCERNS OF MANAGEMENT

No.	Item	Responses			
		Yes	No	N/A	Comments
	Maintenance of Vital Documents				
11.	Have the vital documents and records of the organization been thoroughly analyzed and control procedures set up?				
12.	Does the organization use a remote, safe document storage vault?				
13.	Is there use of Computer Output Microfilm-/Microfiche or the microfilming of documents, and are copies stored in a safe vault?				
14.	Are application and operations documentation of programs handling vital information backed up in safe storage?				
15.	Is the Legal Department satisfied with the EDP handling of vital documents?				
	Protection of Facilities, Equipment, Programs, and Supplies				
16.	Are the organization's Fire, Safety, and Engineering people working closely with Information Services?				
17.	Have the fire and safety systems in the EDP facility area been reviewed by an independent person?				
18.	Have discussions been held with all equipment vendors as to their response to an emergency situation?				
19.	Has there been a recent review as to the documentation level of programs and the existence of updated backup copies of the programs and the documentation?				
20.	Is there a complete listing of all supplies and copies of all forms available in a second site, and are emergency backups of critical forms held in a second site?				

Figure 14-1
(Page 3)

PRIORITY CONCERNS OF MANAGEMENT

No.	Item	Yes	No	N/A	Comments
	Backup Arrangements: On-Site				

21.	Are there contingency plans formalized for three levels of response to trouble:
	  a. delay and correct situation?
	  b. readjust scheduling and use some off-premises equipment?
	  c. shift to backup office site?				

22.	Is the data backup library located in a separately locked room or locked cabinet?				
23.	Are critical program and data files identified and backed up to protect specific systems considered vital to the business?				
24.	Are these backup files continually updated?				
25.	Is the use of files continuously logged?				
26.	Are copies of the computer system operating manuals kept in fireproof storage?				
27.	Is a supply of critical forms kept in a separate building or with the vendor?				
28.	Is a listing of all administrative and technical manuals maintained to assure their identification if lost or stolen?				
29.	Are data programs and system procedures sent for storage in another area?				
	Backup Arrangements: Off-Site				
30.	Have formal reciprocal agreements for backup been made with organizations?				

31.	Do the agreements include specifications as to:
	  a. machine type/model?
	  b. disk units: type and number?
	  c. utilities?
	  d. input procedures?
	  e. available hours for backup processing?				

Figure 14-1
(Page 4)

PRIORITY CONCERNS OF MANAGEMENT

No.	Item	Yes	No	N/A	Comments
	Backup Arrangements: Off-Site (Continued)				
32.	Does the backup facility keep the prime facility aware of any changes made to either hardware or software?				
33.	If the processor or the resources of the backup facility are less than those of the prime facility, have the program changes been taken into account?				
34.	Does the backup facility itself offer satisfactory security?				
35.	Is the backup facility at a reasonable distance?				
36.	Are the available hours for use of the backup system known?				
37.	Is the possible effect on critical schedules known?				
38.	Have the jobs to be operated at the backup site, together with their data on disk, been identified?				
39.	Has a recovery plan been developed with each step assigned to an employee?				
40.	Has the plan been received by the safety department or engineering group, and approved by all involved?				
41.	Has a disaster ever been simulated, with the backup facilities used, as a rehearsal?				

There are three levels of security and disaster recovery measures that should be considered in balancing cost to need. These are:

    a. Mandatory Measures

    b. Necessary Measures

    c. Desirable Measures

● **Mandatory Measures**

Mandatory security and disaster recovery measures are those related to fire control, alarm systems, evacuation procedures, and other emergency precautions necessary to protect the lives and well-being of people in the area involved. Mandatory measures also include those needed to protect the books of account of the organization, and to hold its officers free from legal negligence. The protection must include the assets of the organization as much as possible. The cost of these mandatory measures must be included in the cost of doing business. The items must also be reviewed periodically as to routine operation and adequacy. They should be reviewed with organization counsel.

● **Necessary Measures**

Necessary security and disaster recovery measures include all reasonable precautions taken to prevent serious disruption of the operation of the organization. This will include selected areas of:

    a. Manufacturing and Distribution

    b. Engineering and Planning

    c. Sales and Marketing

    d. Employee Relations, and so on.

The necessity of the measures must be determined by senior management, who should also review their understanding of the need periodically. Since the necessary measures will be included in the base operating cost of the organization, each selected measure must be reviewed as to both degree and speed of emergency backup required.

● **Desirable Measures**

Desirable security and disaster recovery measures include reasonable precautions taken to prevent real inconvenience or disruption to any area of the organization, and to keep the business under smooth control. The cost of some precautions related to personnel is small, but planned action is important to maintain operational efficiency and morale.

    Note: The mandatory measures should be implemented as soon as possible. The necessary measures should be implemented in time-phased, prioritized order, with a definite plan approved by senior management. The desirable measures should be implemented as circumstances allow. Overhead cost is balanced against perceived need and desirability.

- ## Practical Levels of Disaster Recovery Measures

A Disaster Recovery Plan should be specific to the organization and tailored to its needs. An off-the-shelf plan is of no use whatsoever at the time of a security event when individuals need to know exactly what their role is and the steps they must take. The presence of a "paper plan" does not in itself provide a disaster recovery capability. All people in the organization who may be involved in a recovery activity should also be involved in the plan preparation, training, and testing.

14.3   TYPES OF DISASTER TO CONSIDER

No reasonable planning can be done without first reaching an agreement within the organization as to what types of disaster could realistically affect the small computer operation and what are the most probable disaster occurrences to expect.

The various types of disaster to consider include:

a. **Natural Disasters:**

Floods	Earthquakes
Winter Storms	Hurricanes
Forest Fires	Tornadoes

b. **Man-Made Disasters:**

Fires	Burst Pipes
Accidents (Chemical, Transportation)	Building Collapse
Thefts	Bomb Threats
Willful Destruction	Plane Crash
Sabotage	

c. **Political Disasters:**

Riots and Civil Disturbances	Strikes
War	Nuclear Attack

This list should be considered by the management involved, and the necessary response needed should be agreed upon. It will depend upon the area of operation of the organization, the location of the system, and the location of information needs. A disaster could realistically wipe out the need of computer operations if it destroyed most of the organization's operations which are serviced in a limited area. Similarly, some groups will have more concern with earthquakes or hurricanes than will others.

The most likely threats to occur should receive the attention. These disasters may be localized and will be the direct responsibility of the computer management to prepare against. Disasters, such as major building fires or hurricanes, are normally the responsibility of other groups in the company as they are generally too extensive for consideration by data processing personnel only. Concern for the general organization operations will then be overriding. The same procedures to back up the facilities should apply, but there will be less concern with the organization's cash flow from the EDP point of view, and far more concern with the protection of the people and the maintenance of overall organization services.

If an organization is wide-spread, there is considerable incentive to maintain a distant (at least 100 miles) backup site. If an organization is in a narrow geographic area, the backup site could be much closer. In either case, the maintenance of vital records must be in a secure place, regardless of geography. The concept of disaster backup sites for vital records is relatively independent of backup operations sites.

- ## Most Probable Disaster Occurrences

Having agreed on the types of disaster to consider, the study team involved, and management, should analyze the most probable disaster occurrences. If this list is of reasonable length, or if the effects of the occurrences will be different, and are readily grouped, a **disaster recovery scenario** could be written for each type of occurrence, and plans laid for each scenario.

A practical approach, however, is to choose from the list the type of disaster that would be of greatest concern to the computer system area. This can be considered in developing the **Key Disaster Scenario**. Detailed plans could then be laid for it. Normally, the Key Disaster Scenario will focus on an occurrence involving the computer room, or nearby areas. This threat would be of particular concern, because it could concentrate in the computer facility area and not physically affect the rest of the organization. If the computer operation is an integral part of the organization's operations, the effect on financial control and cash flow could be disastrous. A sustained shutdown of the EDP facility, while the rest of the organization is trying to operate normally, would be most serious. The Key Disaster Scenario, and the disaster recovery procedures, should be designed especially to meet this threat.

There are five types of disaster to which Information Services operations could generally be vulnerable. This is an arbitrary list which should be modified by the study. In order of their probability, they are:

   a. **Damage to Individual Terminal Areas:** Fire, water damage, or other destruction in a localized situation in a terminal area is the most probable type of disaster to occur. This could be from common causes, such as electric wiring faults or waste basket burning. It would require some readjustment of the communications, and the establishment of new terminal facilities, depending upon the priority of the operations involved.

   b. **Localized Damage in Data Processing Offices:** Similiar types of disaster to the above become more critical when they occur in the systems, programming, key input, or other areas of the data processing offices. It is likely that such disaster could affect production schedules, systems development work, or general information distribution. Such incidents could also affect a number of different users at the same time, and records could be destroyed that are difficult to replace.

c. **Damage to the EDP Facilities Area:** Substantial fire, water leak, or bomb threat to the computer room represent the most likely serious problems to affect continued operation. The location of the disaster could be more important than the size of the disaster in this case. A relatively small security event could cripple the whole EDP facility. Damage of this type is uniquely the problem of data processing management, and is normally selected as the **Key Disaster Scenario.** Although the most likely problem may be a small electrical fire in a contained area, the effect of it could extend to all users of the computer services, and the response may have to be complete relocation of the computer operation.

d. **Substantial Damage to the Organization's Offices:** Major fire, major flood from burst pipes, or major bomb or riot threat affecting a large part of the organization's offices may affect the EDP facilities simultaneously. In this case there may be little salvageable equipment or space throughout the area. Organization operational problems would take precedence, but it would be up to data processing to recover their operations simultaneously. It would probably have a serious effect on the EDP plans, but the Key Disaster Scenario should still be the basis of the activities to be undertaken.

e. **Regional Damage in a Broad Area:** Extremely heavy storms, floods, hurricanes, or acts of war could affect a broad part of the operating area of the organization. There could be widespread loss of power and telephone lines, disrupted public transportation, and substantial difficulty for employees to report to work.

The Key Disaster Scenario for most companies need not be concerned with acts of war, such as nuclear bombing, widespread hurricane damage and flooding, or particularly severe winter storms. Such disasters will have such an overriding effect on the company's general operations, that EDP recovery will be a minor part of the problems facing management.

●   **Key Disaster Scenario**

There is a critical disaster scenario which is called the **Key Disaster Scenario.** Such a disaster could have a marked effect on the company's operations and profits, and it is necessary that preparations be made in advance for it to minimize its impact. The Key Disaster Scenario will normally call for the full implementation of the Disaster Recovery Plan.

The disaster which triggers the Key Disaster Scenario will likely be a fire, flood, or explosion that occurs in the vicinity of the main computer room, particularly near the communications equipment and lines or the power supply.

A typical Key Disaster Scenario, in brief outline, may be:

a.   A security event occurs in an area close to the computer room at midnight on a Friday. (Note that the majority of disasters which cause great damage occur at night or on weekends.

b.   A night operator or a security guard detects the event, and rings the alarm.   Local Fire and Police departments arrive on the scene.

c.   The person who rang the alarm calls the organization's Security or Building manager, in accordance with the posted instructions in the Guard room.

d.   A person who knows the existence of the EDP Disaster Recovery Plan calls the responsible data processing manager.

e.   The data processing manager comes to the site as rapidly as possible and determines what has happened, and what has already been done by the Fire Department and others.

f.   A decision is made on the extent of the operational needs, the "phone trees" are started, and the Disaster Recovery Plan is put into effect.

14.4   PREPARATION OF AN EDP DISASTER RECOVERY PLAN

Most of the information required should already exist in documented form in the user or EDP areas. It is helpful, at this stage, to make out lists of Requests for Information tailored to each group and distribute them to the appropriate supervisors.

The information is simply basic data on what is involved to give an idea of the size of the problem, the relationships involved, and a few of the facts. **Figure 14-2, Requests for Information,** gives examples of typical lists for these early requests.

Figure 14-2
(Page 1)

REQUESTS FOR INFORMATION

EDP Operations Documentation

1. EDP Facility Layout

   - Site Plan, Floor Plan, and Utility Lines

2. Organization Chart

   - List Names, Addresses, and Telephone Numbers of Supervisors and Staff

3. Hardware Configuration

4. List of Vendors and Contacts

   - Include Miscellaneous Equipment, Data Entry Equipment, Microfilm, etc.

5. Any Emergency Warning Systems, Emergency Controls, or Emergency Communications Systems

6. Any Assigned Responsibilities for Fire, Safety, or Emergency in the User or EDP Departments.

7. Any Emergency and First Aid Equipment

8. Number of Disk, Diskette, and Tape Files.

   - Documentation of what is Duplicated and Off-Site

9. Operating Manuals and Written Procedures

   - Including Powering Down, Emergency Shutdown, Safety Rules, etc.

10. Volumes of Supplies Stored and Approximate Weekly Use

Figure 14-2
(Page 2)

REQUESTS FOR INFORMATION

Application Systems Documentation

1. List of Applications Systems with:

    - Contact Responsibility in EDP and User Departments

    - Processing Requirements and Schedules

      - Number of Terminals Used

    - Program and Data Files

    - Checklist of Documentation

      - List of Programs

      - Control of Documentation

2. List of Development, Maintenance, and Test Work

    - Personnel Assigned

    - Computer Requirements

3. List of Purchased or Leased Application Systems

    - Vendors and Contacts

4. List of Personnel Responsible for Running the Systems

    - Addresses and Telephone Numbers

Figure 14-2
(Page 3)

REQUESTS FOR INFORMATION

Technical Support Documentation

1. Operating System Software

   - Checklist of Documentation and Tapes Required

2. Estimation of Choice of Priority Applications on Backup Computer

3. Review Emergency Possibilities of:

   - Moving Applications to Timesharing Services

   - Moving Applications Batch to Other Computers

   - Other Similar Computers in the Geographic Area

4. Disaster Coordination with Technical Support Group or Database Group

5. List of Vendors and Contacts for Systems

6. List of Technical Support Personnel

   - Addresses and Telephone Numbers

Figure 14-2
(Page 4)

REQUESTS FOR INFORMATION

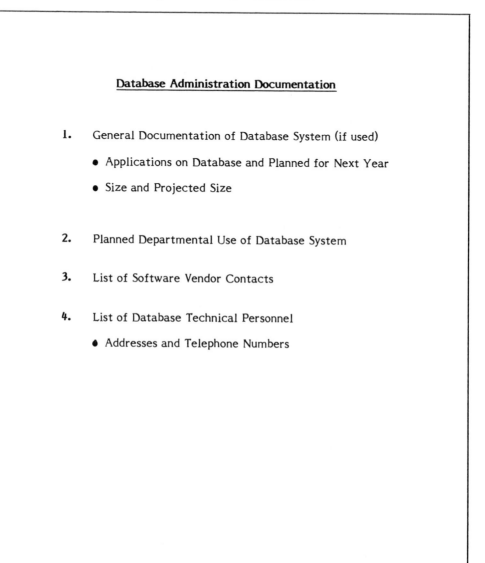

Database Administration Documentation

1. General Documentation of Database System (if used)

    - Applications on Database and Planned for Next Year

    - Size and Projected Size

2. Planned Departmental Use of Database System

3. List of Software Vendor Contacts

4. List of Database Technical Personnel

    - Addresses and Telephone Numbers

Figure 14-2
(Page 5)

REQUESTS FOR INFORMATION

Office Services Documentation

1. Company Policy Statements and Positions

   - Emergencies

   - Security

   - Civil Preparedness

2. Company Emergency Communications Plans

3. Plans for Protection of Vital Records and Documents

4. Company Medical and First Aid Facilities

5. Industry/City Mutual Aid Arrangements

6. Company Repair and Restoration Group

7. Supplies Storage Facilities

8. Lists of:

   - Office Equipment

   - Supplies and Forms (Estimate)

9. List of Key Office Services Personnel

   - Addresses and Telephone Numbers

●　　**EDP Disaster Recovery Project Plan**

If it is desired to have a full EDP Disaster Recovery project, culminating in a comprehensive plan that includes all facets of the EDP operation, the organization and the "plan-for-the-plan" must be carefully assembled. The disaster recovery study project must be handled as any other systems development project and must be broken into phases which are planned for individually. The elements of such a project are provided in **Figure 14-3, EDP Disaster Recovery Project Plan.** This project plan has been designed to divide the effort into six familiar phases for ready reporting to management, and for keeping the study under control.

14.5　　THE EDP DISASTER RECOVERY PLAN

An EDP Disaster Recovery Plan should include:

a.　**The EDP Disaster Recovery Plan Report** outlining all aspects of the plan.

b.　**Recommendations for Actions by Management** to put the plan in place and to test it regularly.

c.　**EDP Disaster Recovery Procedures** giving detailed assignments and locations for actions to be taken at the time of an emergency until the backup operation is running.

d.　**Recovery and Restoration Procedures** to return to the original site or another one selected by management.

e.　**Documentation and Related Information** as an Appendix which may not be included with most copies of the plan.

●　　**Routine Backup Requirements**

Disaster recovery can only be successful if there is a routine backup, at least daily, of the system software, proprietary packages, programs, and data, and there is a regular testing of hardware and communications backup facilities.

Figure 14-4, Routine Backup Requirements, outlines some of the general areas that will have to be considered. Specific, detailed plans must be made in all areas. Most of the routine backup will be daily.

●　　**Disaster Recovery Systems Requirements**

The requirements for the disaster recovery of systems are principally the capabilities of the personnel and equipment to use the routine backup materials in order to reconstruct the data, programs, and conditions of the last successful run before the security event. The Systems staff will be the key to a successful recovery.

Figure 14-3
(Page 1)

EDP DISASTER RECOVERY PROJECT PLAN

I. Definition Phase

1. Decide on disaster recovery objectives

2. Appoint personnel responsible for developing a Disaster Recovery Plan

3. Develop initial set of assumptions and definitions

4. Decide on types of disaster to consider

5. Tentatively select a Key Disaster Scenario

II. Functional Requirements Phase

1. Assemble all organizational procedures and standards relative to emergencies

2. Assemble all documentation relative to the inventory of resources, including hardware, communications, software, forms, facility descriptions, etc.

3. Make an evaluation of what systems are mandatory, necessary, or desirable

4. Analyze the applications and facilities against the recovery objectives

5. Decide on long-term strategy or short-term, high-impact plan

6. Assess the operational requirements of the critical resources and applications

7. Agree on the assumptions and definitions

8. Tentatively determine what is to be covered in the plan

9. Set priorities and acceptable timeframes for recovery

Figure 14-3
(Page 2)

EDP DISASTER RECOVERY PROJECT PLAN

III.   Design and Development Phase

1. Decide on the requirements for the critical resources and applications

2. Evaluate alternative recovery strategies

3. Select one or more specific recovery strategies

4. Perform a cost/benefit analysis for the management report

5. Perform a full risk analysis, if appropriate

6. Decide on the organization for disaster recovery

7. Plan the management of resources during a disaster event

8. Identify potential vendors and price their services

9. Select the final design and prepare detailed recovery procedures

10. Produce the Plan report with recommendations

IV.   Implementation Phase

1. Acquire any hardware, software, communications lines, etc. that are needed

2. Negotiate and sign contracts with vendors

3. Get agreement on final, detailed procedures

4. Train personnel

5. Prepare site

6. Develop test and monitoring plans

7. Develop maintenance plan

Figure 14-3
(Page 3)

EDP DISASTER RECOVERY PROJECT PLAN

V. **Testing and Monitoring Phase**

1. Set up test plan with Internal Audit

2. Schedule tests for small sections of the plan at a time

3. Make arrangements to use facilities external to your organization

4. Attempt to run backup systems

5. Analyze the backup output compared to the normal operations

6. Correct errors in the plan

7. Repeat a variety of tests periodically

VI. **Maintenance Phase**

1. Develop a system to update names, responsibilities, and telephone numbers

2. See that system for backup libraries is working smoothly

3. Standardize documentation and procedures

Figure 14-4

ROUTINE BACKUP REQUIREMENTS

A. **Secure Operating System and All Proprietary Software:**

1. Maintain a central library file of all program products.

2. Routinely dump all necessary software to diskette or tape, and store at a secure site.

3. Use a library management program, if available.

B. **Maintain Adequate File Backup for Application Systems:**

1. Review all operational systems for adequate backup and documentation.

2. Establish a routine backup schedule for all operational systems.

3. Review system file security for all new applications and all modifications.

4. Enforce file security specifications and procedures.

5. Assure that backup files represent the latest data.

C. **Enforce Controlled Library Procedures:**

1. Confirm procedures and responsibility for all tape and disk handling.

2. Maintain separation of functions in handling data files.

3. Assure that all necessary library files are routinely rotated to a secure site.

4. Duplicate and keep off-site all run books and systems control programs.

5. Establish procedures for copying tapes, duplicating microfilm, reading cards to tape, or performing other operations necessary to maintain backup files with the latest available data.

D. **Review Backup and Recovery Procedures with the User Departments:**

1. Determine which files must be backed up.

2. Establish backup responsibility and schedules for each user area.

In moving to a different computer, the greatest problems will be in setting up the job control stream and in operating the computer. It is, therefore, important that:

a. The Systems personnel consider the various possible configurations of the backup system and prepare as much of the job control language in advance as possible; and

b. The Computer Operations Personnel try a number of test runs on the backup computer, using only backup files that would be available in a disaster.

● **Disaster Recovery Hardware and Communications Requirements**

In addition to the preparation of the disaster recovery operations procedures, and the training of the personnel in those procedures, a principal requirement is to have full and detailed documentation stored in a secure site.

There is always a problem of keeping such documentation updated. The best solution is to have as much of it as possible, even the equipment configurations, on a programmed documentation system. It is then readily updated at a terminal, and is always backed up with the routine system library program.

● **Disaster Recovery Personnel Requirements**

The most critical and complex part of the management of resources is in the planning, organization, and training of the required personnel. Experienced, well-trained personnel will scarcely need detailed procedures, but they must be at the right place at the right time, and sure of their assignments. There must be personnel plans for use:

a. **At the Time of Disaster**

b. **For Disaster Recovery**

c. **For Handling Personnel**

The Team can use **Figure 14-5, Personnel Requirements at the Backup Site,** as a worksheet for estimating and planning the assignments of personnel, and planning for space for them at the backup site.

● **Backup Site Planning Requirements**

The backup site is a resource that should be carefully planned. It should be reviewed in as much detail as is normally given to any data center design. Some of the considerations are:

Floor Layout Plans

Environmental Controls

Figure 14-5

PERSONNEL REQUIREMENTS AT THE BACKUP SITE

Personnel	1st Shift Current/Proj/ Essential		2nd Shift Current/Proj/ Essential		3rd Shift Current/Proj/ Essential	
Managers/Supervisors	/	/	/	/	/	/
Systems Analysts/Programmers	/	/	/	/	/	/
Technical Support	/	/	/	/	/	/
Computer Operators	/	/	/	/	/	/
Data Entry	/	/	/	/	/	/
Secretaries/Clerical	/	/	/	/	/	/
Terminal Operators	/	/	/	/	/	/
Communications	/	/	/	/	/	/
Vendor Customer Engineer (CE)	/	/	/	/	/	/
Other:						
_____	/	/	/	/	/	/
_____	/	/	/	/	/	/
_____	/	/	/	/	/	/
_____	/	/	/	/	/	/
Total	/	/	/	/	/	/

Comments: Any pertinent information, such as special procedures for handi-capped etc.

Service and Repair Contacts

Ancillary Equipment

Furniture and Equipment

Supplies

Building Control

Fire and Safety

- **Management and User Agreements on Actions**

When the Detailed Recovery Procedures are in rough draft, they will require approval of both management and users, and they should be reviewed in detail with the personnel who will be expected to carry out the plans. There must be agreements reached in four areas:

a. In the descriptions of the responsibilities and functions of the EDP Disaster Recovery Team.

b. The plan must be confirmed with the user management of the organization.

c. There should be specific agreement that the division of the various Disaster Recovery responsibilities is reasonable and equitable, and does not interfere with regular management of the area.

d. There must be cooperation and agreement among the users in establishing the priorities of operation and the minimum system requirements for the emergency computer system.

After such agreements or decisions have been obtained, the Plan can be finalized, and presented formally to all who may be concerned.

- **Vendor Agreements**

Most equipment vendors have a policy that, if a disaster hits one of their systems on rent, they will take the next one off the line or on the shipping dock to replace their equipment, and they will transport it to the site by the fastest available means. Experience has proven that most vendors will send along a team of systems engineers and installers who will work around-the-clock to help the user recover from the disaster. If the facility has mixed-vendor equipment, they will have to bring in all the vendors. Experience has proven that most vendors will work cooperatively and hard to bring up a mixed-vendor installation rapidly.

It is worthwhile to contact all vendors, despite their published policies, and discuss the ramifications with their local salesman and sales manager.

The Telephone Company should be included in the vendor discussions.

14.6   THE ACTION PLAN

When there has been sufficient analysis of the problem, and the management of the resources has been planned for the key scenarios, the EDP Disaster Recovery Procedures can be assembled. These constitute the Action Plan. They tell specific individuals, or positions, what their responsibilities are and what actions to take. They tell the Who, What, When, and Where, with little discussion of the Why. When an emergency strikes, people should be able to take the Disaster Recovery Procedures and follow their own sections, confident that they are working in concert with the rest of the team.

An example of an outline of an EDP Disaster Recovery Plan for a small computer system is provided in **Figure 14-6, EDP Disaster Recovery Plan.** It has been arbitrarily divided into three phases.

Phase I: Initial Response

Phase II: Disaster Recovery at Backup Site

Phase III: Recovery at Original or Alternate Site

This cannot be a detailed, fill-in-the-blanks plan, because each organization will have unique requirements, and will have developed their own strategies. In addition, the majority of activities will take place in parallel by the different recovery teams, coordinated by management. Also, the recovery times after the disaster event will vary depending on the need of the organization and the preparations that have been made. The major steps, and the principles illustrated, will be valid for all, however.

The Action Plan Procedures must be simple listings with little explanation. The use of "Playscript Procedure" writing can be helpful for the overlapping activities. Key actions must be in the front of each section and highlighted.

A separate list of actions can be developed and maintained for each of the major problem scenarios considered possible. For example, different responses may be required for bomb threats, fires, serious power outages, and so forth. The list of people, of course, will remain the same, and many of the actions will be the same. For most computer centers, a single list of actions will be sufficient with management selecting and giving appropriate orders.

Copies of the instructions must be readily available when a disaster occurs as will be discussed.

● **Phase I: Initial Response**

The **Emergency Response Procedures** are started as soon as a disaster is recognized. This may be after a fire alarm has been pulled, and the organization's emergency departments have been alerted.

Figure 14-6
(Page 1)

EDP DISASTER RECOVERY PLAN

PHASE I

Initial Response

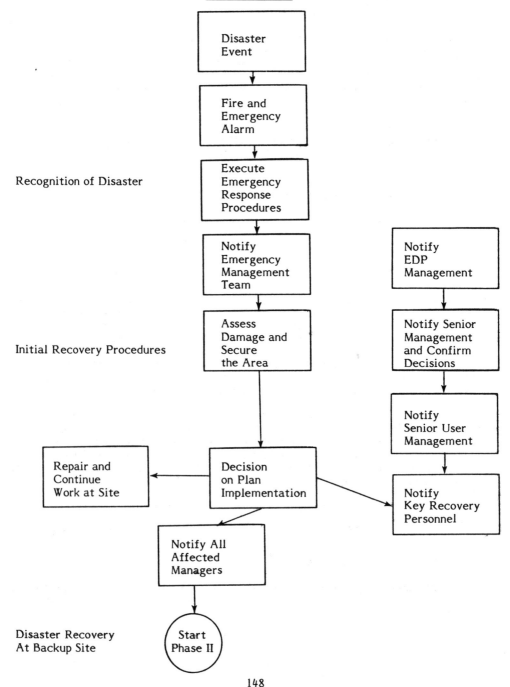

Figure 14-6
(Page 2)

EDP DISASTER RECOVERY PLAN

PHASE II

Disaster Recovery at Backup Site

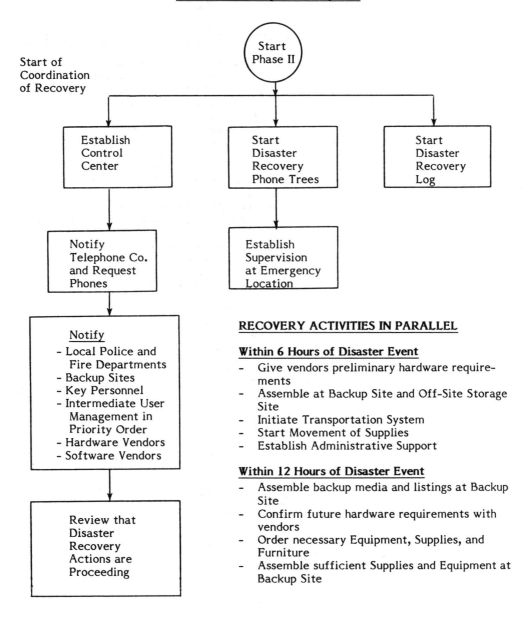

Start of
Coordination
of Recovery

Start
Phase II

Establish
Control
Center

Start
Disaster
Recovery
Phone Trees

Start
Disaster
Recovery
Log

Notify
Telephone Co.
and Request
Phones

Establish
Supervision
at Emergency
Location

Notify
- Local Police and
  Fire Departments
- Backup Sites
- Key Personnel
- Intermediate User
  Management in
  Priority Order
- Hardware Vendors
- Software Vendors

Review that
Disaster
Recovery
Actions are
Proceeding

RECOVERY ACTIVITIES IN PARALLEL

Within 6 Hours of Disaster Event
- Give vendors preliminary hardware requirements
- Assemble at Backup Site and Off-Site Storage Site
- Initiate Transportation System
- Start Movement of Supplies
- Establish Administrative Support

Within 12 Hours of Disaster Event
- Assemble backup media and listings at Backup Site
- Confirm future hardware requirements with vendors
- Order necessary Equipment, Supplies, and Furniture
- Assemble sufficient Supplies and Equipment at Backup Site

Phase II Continued

149

Figure 14-6
(Page 3)

EDP DISASTER RECOVERY PLAN

PHASE II (Continued)

Disaster Recovery at Backup Site

RECOVERY ACTIVITIES IN PARALLEL (Continued)

Within 24 Hours of Disaster Event
- Restore system pack and test system
- Start operation of critical systems
- Have Backup Site stocked and operating
- Have transportation system working for necessary people and supplies
- Bring up Operating System
- Bring up and test Database, if any
- Test and debug systems
- Have all critical application systems operational
- Establish processing schedule
- Inventory application systems availability at site
- Notify all concerned users
- Inventory salvageable material
- Reassess damage
- Debrief staff and report to management

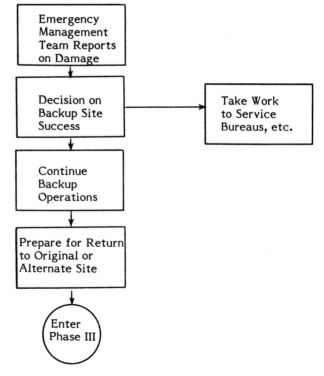

Figure 14-6
(Page 4)

EDP DISASTER RECOVERY PLAN

PHASE III

Recovery At Original or Alternate Site

- Decisions on recovery timing and equipment
- Site preparation
- Development of recovery procedures in reverse direction
- Repeat of recovery procedures
- Bring up all systems
- Report to management
- Debrief Staff

- ## Phase II: Disaster Recovery at Backup Site

    As soon as a disaster has been declared, key people will be called to start the Disaster Recovery telephone trees to get them all in action.   The Emergency Management Team will establish a Control Center and start the coordination of the recovery. Disaster Recovery Logs will be started by the management team and each of the other teams so that there is a trail of the actions taken.

    A great many activities will then be started in parallel.   These will depend upon the particular organization. Some examples are noted in Figure 14-6.

- ## Phase III: Recovery at Original or Alternate Site

    While operations are running at the backup site, plans must be made for full recovery at the original site.

- ## EDP Disaster Recovery Procedures Manual

    The planning required for the preparation of an EDP Disaster Recovery Plan should culminate in a final report and a brief, written manual, EDP Disaster Recovery Procedures. This is a working document, giving the "Who, What, When, and Where" as described above. It is a portion of the final report.

    The suggested sections for the EDP Disaster Recovery Procedures are:

    1.   EDP Disaster Recovery Procedures

    2.   Initial Disaster Response

    3.   Computer Room Emergency Procedures

    4.   EDP Disaster Recovery Actions

    5.   Emergency Assignments and Locations

    6.   Emergency Vendor Contacts

    7.   Disaster Recovery Log

    8.   Organization Charts and Facilities Plans

- ## Producing the Final Report

    The final report will be the full EDP Disaster Recovery Plan. **Figure 14-7, Outline of Final Report, EDP Disaster Recovery Plan,** lists typical topics which should be addressed in the plan report. Particular care should be paid to the Overview and the Recommendations, as they are likely to be all that is thoroughly read by senior management. Much of the rest will be detailed and technical.

Figure 14-7
(Page 1)

OUTLINE OF FINAL REPORT
EDP DISASTER RECOVERY PLAN

I. <u>MANAGEMENT OVERVIEW</u>

- Purpose and Objectives
- Scope and Applicability
- Assumptions and Definitions
- Responsibilities and Approvals
- Strategies Considered
- Strategies Selected

II. <u>REQUIRED DISASTER RECOVERY PREPARATIONS</u>

- People (Assignments, Responsibilities, Training)
- Sites (Selection, Environmental Preparation)
- Software Systems (Inventory, Backup, Responsibility)
- Application Systems (Inventory, Backup, Responsibility)
- Data and Databases (Inventory, Backup, Handling)
- Hardware (Inventory, Emergency, Agreements, Documentation)
- Communications (Current, Backup, Planned Requirements)
- Transportation (Emergency Requirements)
- Supplies (Lists of Critical Items, Vendors, Stocks)
- Documentation (Inventory, Off-Site Backup)
- Other Equipment (Data Input, COM, Copiers, etc.)
- Vendor Contracts or Letters of Understanding
- Test Plans

Figure 14-7
(Page 2)

OUTLINE OF FINAL REPORT

EDP DISASTER RECOVERY PLAN

III. **EDP DISASTER RECOVERY PROCEDURES: THE ACTION PLAN**

- Emergency Response and Initial Recovery Procedures
- Disaster Recovery at Backup Site
- Recovery at Original or Alternate Site

IV. **RECOMMENDATIONS**

- Summary of Cost of Plan
- Summary of Time Schedule of Plan
- Recommendation for Staged Development of the Plan
- Immediate Actions to be Taken
- Expenditures to be Made in Priority Order

- **Recommendations for Action**

The Recommendations for Action are of great importance to EDP management and, therefore, must be emphasized.

The Recommendations for Action should be carefully grouped for timing and importance. If they are accepted, the funding may be all at once, or it may be phased. EDP management must be sure of their priorities for the recommendations.

- **Restoration of the Permanent Facility**

Restoration of the permanent facility is a substantive part of the EDP Disaster Recovery Plan, but it can seldom be planned and rehearsed in detail in advance. Restoration of the permanent facility should, therefore, be discussed and considered in generality. The details should be left to the time of need, however, unless decisions have been made in advance about moving to a new permanent site. Such action is not avoiding the issue, since the detailed procedures for the recovery teams that have been carefully thought through will normally be usable in reverse for the final recovery action.

SECTION 15

RELATED REFERENCES

(Selected by Permission from "Quarterly Bibliography of
Computers and Data Processing," Applied Computer Research,
P.O. Box 9280, Phoenix, Arizona)

BOOKS AND REPORTS

EDP Disaster Recovery: Planning, Implementation, and Procedures. FTP, 1981-3 Vols.,
Variable paging. $275.00.

> A loose-leaf reference service covering the planning, management, and
> installation of an EDP disaster recovery plan. Management and personnel
> participation in recovery planning is discussed, and a procedures manual is
> included. Updated periodically.

Security: Data, Facility, and Personnel. FTP. 1982-. Variable paging. 2 Vols.
$375.00.

> A loose-leaf reference service written for the internal auditor and/or manage-
> ment's use in measuring adequacy of security in an EDP organization. Planning
> and implementation of EDP security measures are outlined. A checklist format
> covers both management and technical considerations, including backup
> arrangements, company security, insurance, vital records security, physical
> security, personnel considerations, software considerations, operations
> considerations, and data communications. Sections are also included on costs,
> security hardware and a bibliography. Updated periodically.

Security Evaluator. FTP. 1980. Variable paging. $125.00.

> A loose-leaf reference service designed to measure the adequacy and
> effectiveness of an organization's security status. A series of questionnaires
> are used to evaluate system internal controls, input and output controls, on-
> line systems controls, fire and physical protection, personnel policies, use of
> outside services, and insurance coverage. An analysis of security costs is also
> included. Updated periodically.

Steinmetz, Jay Stephen, **Secure Computer Network,** NTIS, NOV 82. 114 pp. AD-A124
820/2. $13.00.

> Develops the initial design for a secure computer network and presents the
> concepts of physical security reference monitors, encryption, and network
> protocols.

PERIODICALS

A Question of Leadership. DATMATION 29:119-20 +, FEB 83

Discusses data security programs and problems including dealing with non-DP professionals, balancing user-friendliness with security, and confronting information security rather than just computer security.

Ball, Leslie D. et al., **Disaster Recovery Services.** COMP & SEC 1:216-25. NOV 82.

Reviews services of disaster recovery planning vendors to provide fully configured service centers, empty shells, and cooperative arrangements. 19 references.

Blom, Rolf, et al., **On Security Measures in Distributed Computer Systems.** COMP & SEC 1:113-22. JUN 82.

Studies basic problems of data security: discusses protection of databases, designating addressees and authorization to access data and messages, and requirements for equipment in a local net environment. 22 references.

Bussolati, U. and Martella, G., **Data Security Management in Distributed Databases.** INFO-SYSTEMS 7: No. 3:217-27. 1982.

Analyzes the problem of Data Security Management in a Distrubuted Database made up of an aggregation of heterogeneous Local Databases. 21 references.

Callaghan, David R., **Securing the Distrubuted Word Processing Network.** COMP & SEC 2: No.1:78-81. 1983.

Contends that the weakest configuration in distributed word processing systems is in moderate size networks and that physical security for each terminal or a more sophisticated authorization routine is needed. 4 references.

Casey, Carolyn and Lyons, Michael L., **Technical Reviews for Effective Data Security.** BANK ADMIN 58:22-3. DEC 82.

Contends that the review of systems designs, program modifications, and system testing can provide the separation of responsibilities necessary for controlling data processing in financial institutions.

Courtney, Robert H. Jr., **A Systematic Approach to Data Security.** COMP & SEC 1:99-112. JUN 82.

Describes the basic concept and outline of a systematic approach for selecting internal controls, known as security measures, in a data processing environment, presents data security as a people problem. 15 references.

Defending Your Computer Room Against Disaster. MOD OFF 28:100+. MAR 83.

Contends that a plan is needed to protect data processing facilities from disaster and that a backup procedure is needed to take over when a facility is out of commission.

Goldberg, Michael., **The Data Security Issue.** DATABASE NEWS 10:3-4. NOV/DEC 82.

Introduces basic issues in data security, discusses security administration, and analyzes the security issue in the IMS DB/DC environment.

Guynes, Steve, Laney, Michael G., and Zant, Robert., **Computer Security Practice.** J SYS MGMT 34-22-6. JUN 83.

Reviews a survey conducted with the purpose of determining the current computer security plans and procedures being used.

Haliday, Wallace. G., **Multics Handles Security in Multi-User Systems.** CAN DATA SYS 15:48-9, FEB 83.

Reports on Honeywell's Multics as a secure, expandable system primarily for use with remote workstations.

Highland, Esther Harris and Highland, Harold Joseph., **A Guide to NBS Computer Security Literature.** COMP & SEC 1:164-76. JUN 82.

Provides a bibliography of special reports and technical studies in the field of computer security that have been published by the U.S. National Bureau of Standards.

Johnson, Bob., **DP "Hacking" Seen as Addiction to be Squelched.** COMPWRLD 17:32, APR 18, 83.

Contends that hacking, an attempt to gain unauthorized access to a computer system, will continue to plague the computer industry.

Malvik, Chip., **Security and the Home Computer.** INFO AGE 5:87-90. APR 83.

Explains why cryptographic techniques should be used for data protection and the use of the public-key cryptosystem, and provides some cryptographic terminology and techniques. 9 references.

Menkus, Belden., **Security Must Be Designed In, Not Added On.** SOFT NEWS 2:21-2, NOV 1, 82.

Contends that software design must be more careful to include security measures within their products.

Multiuser Systems Need Fail-Safe Data Security. COMPWRLD 17:SR 11, MAR 28, 83.

Discusses disadvantages of multiuser systems including the need to provide some form of data security, a tendency in some configuration for reduction in speed as the number of users increases, and a necessity for a fail-safe mechanism.

Murray, William Hugh., **Security Procedures for Program Libraries.** COMP & SEC 1:201-9, NOV 82.

Describes an implementation of procedures, libraries, and separation of duties to improve security in programming, and helps to limit scope, reveal programmer intent, and fix accountability.

Wallach, Gloria T., **Controls Prevent Computer Negligence and Fraud.** J SYS MGMT 34-30-2, MAY 83.

Contends that computer security controls are essential in reducing the opportunities for anyone to perpetrate fraud and in increasing the likelihood that fraudulent activities will be detected.

Waring, L.P., **The Security of Data Communications Systems.** INFO AGE 5:97-104, APR 83.

Describes the potential security threats that face the data communications systems, the way the threats may arise, and the measures that can be taken to counter them.

Wood, Charles Cresson., **Effective Information System Security with Password Controls.** COMP & SEC 2:No.1-5-10, 1983.

Explores some aspects of password system design, including objectives of password controls, design philosophies, man-machine interface design, system administration, and technical system implementation.

Weights, Philip J., **A Methodology for Evaluating Computer Contingency Planning.** EDPACS 10:1-7. OCT 82.

Emphasizes the importance of adequate computer contingency planning based on a disastrous fire which claimed many lives and destroyed a portion of the data processing department.

Wong, Ken., **Quantifying Computer Security Risks and Safeguards: An Actuarial Approach.** 10:1-7. OCT 82.

Defines risk areas and potential losses in relation to computer security and contingency planning. The benefits of carrying out a business impact review are emphasized, and methods of assessing and controlling risks are described.